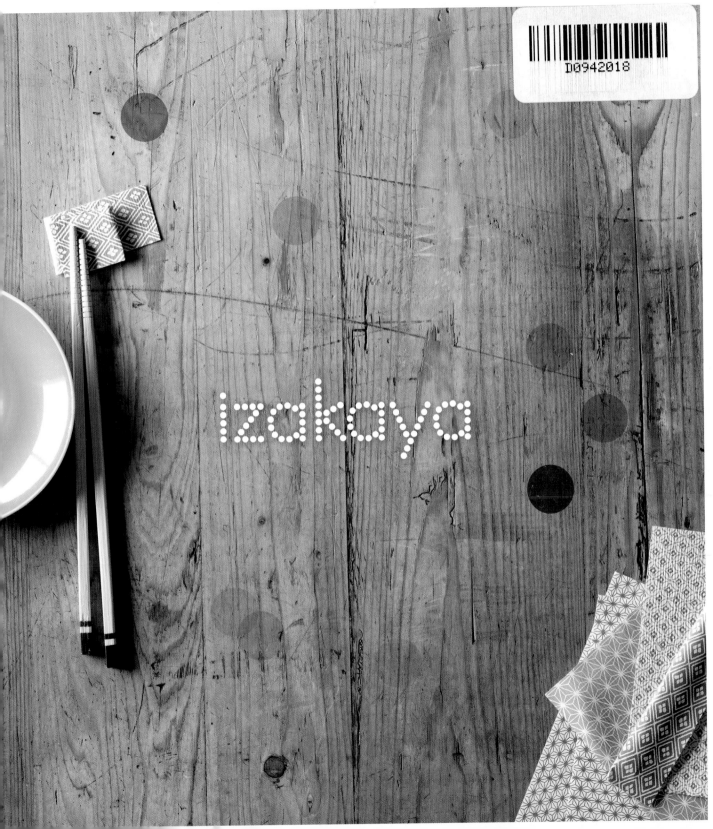

izakaya

izakaya

japanese bar food

hardie grant books
MELBOURNE · LONDON

contents

izakaya!	7
small plates	8
salads	48
skewers	72
sharing plates	110
sweets	148
glossary	168
index	172

izakaya!

Walk beneath the paper lantern, pull back the half curtain and enter a world that suddenly feels like the real Japan. Waiters boisterously welcome you through the door and call out orders to the kitchen. People sit on tatami mats sipping glasses of beer or small cups of sake, chatting about work, family, life. It's relaxed, welcoming and not bound by dizzying rules of etiquette.

This is the traditional izakaya – the Japanese tavern, where the alcohol flows but simple and delicious food is every bit as important. The food comes in small serves designed to nibble on and share. Created from the words '*i*' (to sit or remain) and '*sakaya*' (sake shop), izakayas originated as simple liquor stores that began to serve food to busy working men in the developing city of Edo, now Tokyo. In the last few decades, the izakaya has received a good dusting off, and while you can still find traditional izakayas not much bigger than a shoebox with a bar and wooden shelving to the ceiling, there are now many slick modern establishments and popular izakaya chains.

Classic izakaya dishes include sashimi, edamame (salted fresh soy beans), yakitori (grilled skewers) and agedashi tofu – a dish of deep-fried silken tofu served in a dashi-based broth. Some izakayas specialise in one particular dish, such as tempura or grilled fish, and the specials board is always a guide to the best morsels on offer.

Many izakaya menus feature relaxed Japanese interpretations of Western dishes, such as *korokke* (croquettes) or potato salad in mayonnaise. Ingredients like cheese, butter and bacon sit comfortably alongside miso, soba noodles and nori as the foods that Japanese people love. This hybrid cuisine is so established in Japan that it has its own name – *yoshoku* – including anything from spaghetti to *hambagu* (yes, hamburger!).

Like Japanese food in general, this collection of classic izakaya recipes is guided by the principles of direct flavours, quality ingredients and pleasing presentation. You won't need oodles of ingredients to cook these dishes, or a whole kitchen full of equipment and utensils. Just get out your wok, dust off your barbecue hotplate, arm yourself with some miso and sake, and discover the exciting world of izakaya-style cooking.

small plates

lotus chips

oil, for frying
200 g (7 oz) lotus root, peeled
    and thinly sliced

salt, to serve
ichimi powder, to serve

Pour enough oil into a wok or deep frying pan to come one-third of the way up the side and place over high heat until shimmering. Cook the lotus root, in batches, for 3–5 minutes, or until golden.

Drain on paper towel and sprinkle with the salt and ichimi powder to serve.

Serves 4

japanese pickles

2 tablespoons Japanese rice
    vinegar
1 tablespoon caster (superfine)
    sugar
1 teaspoon Japanese soy sauce
1 teaspoon finely chopped ginger

½ Lebanese (short) cucumber,
    sliced lengthways into
    ½ cm (¼ in) thick strips
    and seeded
3 baby carrots, mixed colours,
    sliced into ½ cm (¼ in)
    rounds

Combine the vinegar, sugar, soy sauce and ginger in a small bowl and stir to dissolve the sugar.

Put the cucumber and carrot in a serving bowl. Pour over the vinegar mixture and cover with plastic wrap. Place in the fridge for 4 hours, stirring occasionally, to allow the flavours to develop. If desired, drain off extra liquid before serving.

Serves 4

oysters with japanese dressing

dressing
2 teaspoons Japanese soy sauce
1 teaspoon mirin
2 teaspoons Japanese rice
  vinegar
½ teaspoon caster (superfine)
  sugar

2 teaspoons dried shredded
  wakame
12 oysters, on the shell
50 g (1¾ oz) salmon roe

To make the dressing, combine all the ingredients in a small bowl.

Soak the wakame in a bowl of cold water for 5 minutes, or until soft. Drain well.

Arrange the oysters on a serving plate and spoon some roe onto each oyster. Spoon over the dressing and some wakame to serve.

Serves 4

spinach with sesame

2 tablespoons toasted sesame
seeds
2 tablespoons dashi stock
1 tablespoon Japanese soy
sauce

1 teaspoon caster (superfine)
sugar
1 teaspoon mirin
1 bunch English spinach,
ends trimmed

Place the sesame seeds in a suribachi or mortar and pound
until the seeds start to break up. Gradually add the dashi stock,
pounding as you go, until the mixture is smooth. Stir in the soy
sauce, sugar and mirin.

Bring a large saucepan of salted water to the boil. Add the spinach
and cook for 3 minutes, or until wilted. Drain and plunge into iced
water. Drain again, then squeeze to remove any excess water.

Place the spinach on a sushi mat and roll tightly. Cut into even
pieces and drizzle with the sesame sauce to serve.

Serves 2

crumbed prawns

12 raw prawns (shrimp), peeled,
  deveined and tails intact
35 g (1¼ oz/¼ cup) plain
  (all-purpose) flour
2 eggs, lightly beaten

60 g (2¼ oz/1 cup) panko
  (Japanese breadcrumbs)
oil, for frying
ponzu sauce (page 66), to serve

Use a sharp knife to make three incisions on the underside of the prawns.

Put the flour, egg and panko in separate bowls. Dust the prawns in the flour, dip in the egg, then coat with the panko.

Pour enough oil into a wok or deep frying pan to come 5 cm (2 in) up the side and place over high heat until shimmering. Add the prawns and cook for 1½ minutes on each side, or until cooked through.

Drain on paper towel and serve with the ponzu sauce.

Serves 4

green beans with miso

miso sauce
3 tablespoons white miso
1 teaspoon caster (superfine)
    sugar
2 tablespoons sake
½ teaspoon Japanese soy
    sauce
5 drops of sesame oil

150 g (5½ oz) baby green
    beans, trimmed

To make the miso sauce, combine all the ingredients in a small
bowl along with 2 tablespoons of water.

Bring a large saucepan of salted water to the boil. Add the beans
and cook for 2 minutes, or until just tender. Drain and plunge into a
bowl of iced water. Drain again.

Transfer the beans to a bowl. Add the miso sauce, toss to combine
and serve.

Serves 4

fried pork stuffed with cheese

2 x 100 g (3½ oz) pork loin fillets
40 g (1½ oz) gruyere cheese
2 tablespoons plain (all-purpose)
    flour
1 egg, lightly beaten
30 g (1 oz/½ cup) panko
    (Japanese breadcrumbs)

2 tablespoons oil
cabbage leaves, cut into
    squares, to serve
tonkatsu sauce, optional,
    to serve

Slice each pork fillet in half horizontally, without cutting all the way through. Open out and use a meat mallet to flatten out slightly. Slice the gruyere in half and place a piece on one side of each pork fillet. Fold over to enclose.

Put the flour, egg and panko into separate bowls. Dust the pork in the flour, dip in the egg, then coat with the panko.

Heat the oil in a frying pan over medium heat and cook the pork for 4 minutes on each side, or until golden and cooked through.

Thickly slice the pork on the diagonal and serve on a bed of cabbage leaves with the tonkatsu sauce, if desired.

Serves 2

fried squid with lemon and salt

....

2 tablespoons plain (all-purpose)
   flour
1 egg, lightly beaten
40 g (1½ oz/⅔ cup) panko
   (Japanese breadcrumbs)

150 g (5½ oz) cleaned squid,
   cut into 1 cm (½ in) rings
oil, for frying
½ tablespoon salt
½ lemon, halved and thinly
   sliced

Put the flour, egg and panko in separate bowls. Dust the squid in the flour, dip in the egg, then coat with the panko.

Pour enough oil into a wok or deep frying pan to come one-third of the way up the side and place over high heat until shimmering. Add the squid and cook for 30 seconds on each side, or until lightly golden. Remove and drain on paper towel.

Place the salt in a bowl, top with the lemon slices and serve alongside the squid. The idea is to squeeze over the lemon and sprinkle with the salt.

Serves 2

crumbed asparagus

12 asparagus spears
60 g (2¼ oz/½ cup) cornflour
  (cornstarch)
60 g (2¼ oz/1 cup) panko
  (Japanese breadcrumbs)

2 eggs, lightly beaten
canola oil, for frying
ponzu sauce (page 66),
  to serve

Snap or cut the woody ends from the asparagus. Bring a saucepan of lightly salted water to the boil. Add the asparagus and cook for 1 minute, or until just tender and emerald green. Drain and put the asparagus into a bowl of chilled water until cool. Drain well.

Put the cornflour and panko on two separate plates. Roll each asparagus spear in the cornflour. Dip into the egg, then roll in the panko until evenly coated all over.

Half fill a frying pan with the oil and place over high heat until the surface of the oil is shimmering. Cook the asparagus for 2 minutes, rolling the spears over in the oil, or until cooked and golden all over.

Drain the asparagus on paper towel and serve with the ponzu sauce on the side for dipping.

Serves 4

vegetable and prawn fritters

dipping sauce
80 ml (2½ fl oz/⅓ cup) dashi
  stock
2 tablespoons Japanese soy
  sauce
2 tablespoons mirin
½ teaspoon caster (superfine)
  sugar

50 g (1¾ oz/⅓ cup) plain
  (all-purpose) flour
2 tablespoons potato flour
160 ml (5¼ fl oz/⅔ cup) iced
  water
100 g (3½ oz) sweet potato,
  peeled and julienned
6 raw prawns (shrimp), peeled,
  deveined and roughly
  chopped
½ small onion, thinly sliced
oil, for frying
salt

To make the dipping sauce, combine all the ingredients in a small bowl.

Combine the flours in a bowl. Gradually add the iced water and stir until combined. Stir through the sweet potato, prawns and onion.

Pour enough oil into a wok or deep frying pan to come 5 cm (2 in) up the side and place over medium–high heat until shimmering. Drop 80 ml (2½ fl oz/⅓ cup) of the mixture into the oil. Cook for 2–3 minutes on each side, or until golden and cooked through.

Drain on paper towel, season with the salt and serve with the dipping sauce.

Serves 4

tempura cheese-stuffed chillies

8 long red chillies
80 g (2¾ oz) cheddar cheese,
    cut into thin strips
80 g (2¾ oz/½ cup) plain
    (all-purpose) flour
2 tablespoons potato flour

160 ml (5¼ fl oz/⅔ cup)
    iced water
oil, for frying
2 tablespoons plain
    (all-purpose) flour, extra
Japanese soy sauce, to serve

Slice the chillies in half lengthways, keeping the stalk intact. Use a small, sharp knife to remove the seeds. Divide the cheese among the chillies and enclose.

Combine the flours in a small bowl. Add the iced water and stir until just combined but still lumpy.

Pour enough oil into a small frying pan to come 2 cm (¾ in) up the side and place over high heat until shimmering. Working quickly, dust the chillies in the extra flour, then coat in the batter. Add to the oil and cook, turning, for 2 minutes, or until lightly golden and crisp.

Drain on paper towel and serve with the soy sauce.

Serves 4

deep-fried eggplant sandwiches

dipping sauce
80 ml (2½ fl oz/⅓ cup) dashi stock
2 tablespoons Japanese soy sauce
2 tablespoons mirin
½ teaspoon caster (superfine) sugar

60 g (2¼ oz) minced (ground) chicken
2 teaspoons Japanese soy sauce
1 spring onion (scallion), thinly sliced
1 teaspoon finely grated ginger

2 teaspoons potato flour
8 slices Japanese eggplant, about
    3 mm (⅛ in) thick
2 tablespoons potato flour, extra,
    to dust
oil, for frying
salt
shiso leaves, to garnish
Japanese chilli sauce, optional,
    to serve

To make the dipping sauce, combine all the ingredients in a bowl.

Combine the chicken, soy sauce, spring onion and ginger in a bowl. Mix the potato flour with 2 teaspoons of water in a small jug. Add to the chicken mixture and stir to combine.

Take four slices of eggplant and spread 1 tablespoon of the chicken mixture onto each one. Top with the remaining eggplant. Coat in the extra potato flour.

Pour enough oil into a frying pan to come 5 cm (2 in) up the side and place over medium–high heat until shimmering. Add the eggplant sandwiches and cook for 2 minutes on each side, or until golden and cooked through.

Drain on paper towel and season with the salt. Sprinkle with the shiso leaves and serve with the dipping sauce and chilli sauce, if desired.

Serves 4

sweet egg omelette

4 eggs, lightly beaten
2 tablespoons dashi stock
2 teaspoons Japanese soy sauce
2 teaspoons mirin
1 teaspoon caster (superfine)
   sugar

oil, for frying
nori, cut into 4 x 1 cm (½ in)
   strips
salmon roe or pickled ginger,
   to serve

Place the eggs in a bowl with the dashi stock, soy sauce, mirin and sugar. Whisk well to combine.

Brush a small non-stick frying pan with the oil and place over medium heat. Pour one-third of the egg mixture into the pan and swirl to coat the base. Cook for 1–2 minutes, or until nearly cooked. Run a spatula around the edge of the pan to loosen, then gently roll up the omelette and remove from the pan.

Repeat the above procedure to make two more omelettes with the remaining mixture.

Transfer the omelettes one at a time to a bamboo sushi mat and roll tightly. Trim the edges and cut into four pieces. Wrap a strip of nori around each roll and top with the salmon roe or pickled ginger.

Serves 4

grilled beef stuffed with asparagus

marinade
60 ml (2 fl oz/¼ cup) sake
2 tablespoons Japanese soy sauce
1 tablespoon mirin
2 teaspoons caster (superfine) sugar

6 asparagus spears, trimmed to 15 cm
  (6 in)
2 x 180 g (6 oz) fillet steaks
2 teaspoons oil

To make the marinade, combine all the ingredients in a jug. Stir to dissolve the sugar, then set aside.

Bring a deep frying pan of water to a simmer. Add the asparagus and cook for 3 minutes, or until just tender. Rinse well under cold running water.

Slice each steak in half horizontally. Use a meat mallet to pound into 15 cm (6 in) pieces, each one about 2 mm (¹/₁₆ in) thick.

Place two pieces of beef on a piece of plastic wrap so that they slightly overlap. Place three asparagus spears across the beef and roll from the short end using the plastic wrap as a guide. Twist each end of the plastic tightly and place in the fridge for 1 hour. Repeat this process with the remaining beef and asparagus.

Remove the beef from the plastic wrap. Add it to the marinade and place in the fridge for 2 hours. Remove the beef from the marinade and pat dry with paper towel.

Heat the oil in a non-stick frying pan over medium–high heat. Add the beef and cook, turning, for 5 minutes, or until browned. Add the marinade and simmer for 2 minutes, or until reduced.

Transfer the beef rolls to a chopping board and slice each one in half. Drizzle over the pan juices to serve.

Serves 2

deep-fried oysters with tonkatsu

12 oysters, on the shell
60 g (2¼ oz/½ cup) cornflour
   (cornstarch)
2 eggs, lightly beaten

30 g (1 oz/½ cup) panko
   (Japanese breadcrumbs)
oil, for frying
tonkatsu sauce, to serve
lemon wedges, to serve

Slip the oysters from their shells and place on two layers of paper towel for 5 minutes before cooking. Rinse and dry the shells, then set aside.

Put the cornflour, eggs and panko in three separate bowls. Working one at a time, toss each oyster in the cornflour, dip in the egg, then roll in the panko to coat all over.

Pour in enough oil to reach 2 cm (¾ in) up the side of a frying pan and place over high heat. When the surface of the oil is shimmering, add the oysters and cook for about 30 seconds, or until golden.

Drain on paper towel, then return the oysters to their shells. Serve with the tonkatsu sauce and lemon wedges on the side.

Serves 4

camembert tempura

110 g (3¾ oz/¾ cup) plain (all-purpose) flour
30 g (1 oz/¼ cup) potato flour
¼ teaspoon baking powder
large pinch of salt

325 ml (11 fl oz/2⅓ cups) iced water
100 g (3½ oz) camembert cheese
35 g (1¼ oz/¼ cup) plain (all-purpose) flour, extra
oil, for frying

Sift both of the flours, baking powder and salt into a bowl. Place in the fridge to chill for 30 minutes.

Cut the camembert into ½ cm (¼ in) thick slices. Put the extra flour into a bowl. Toss each piece of camembert in the flour and gently press to coat all over. Set aside.

Half fill a small saucepan with the oil and place over high heat until the surface of the oil is shimmering.

Working quickly, add the iced water to the chilled flour mixture. Use chopsticks to combine, being careful not to overbeat – the mixture should be quite thin and a little lumpy.

Add several pieces of camembert to the batter and use chopsticks to coat the cheese all over. Shake off any excess batter. Add the camembert to the oil and fry for 2 minutes, or until lightly golden and crispy.

Drain on paper towel and repeat the process with the remaining camembert. Serve immediately.

Serves 2

chicken nanban

180 ml (5½ fl oz/¾ cup) dashi
  stock
60 ml (2 fl oz/¼ cup) Japanese rice
  vinegar
2 tablespoons Japanese soy sauce
1 tablespoon caster (superfine)
  sugar
½ white onion, thinly sliced

2 long red chillies, seeded and
  thinly sliced
250 g (9 oz) boneless, skinless
  chicken breast, cut into
  3 cm (1¼ in) pieces
35 g (1¼ oz/¼ cup) potato
  flour
2 tablespoons oil
steamed rice, to serve

Combine the dashi stock, vinegar, soy sauce and sugar in a small saucepan and place over medium heat. Bring to the boil, stirring to dissolve the sugar, then simmer for about 5 minutes, or until slightly thickened. Add the onion and chilli and set aside.

Lightly coat the chicken with the potato flour. Shake off the excess.

Heat the oil in a large frying pan. Add the chicken and cook, turning, for 5–7 minutes, or until golden and cooked through.

Drain the chicken on paper towel and transfer to a heatproof bowl. Pour over the hot dashi mixture. Set aside for 2 hours to allow the flavours to develop.

Serve the chicken at room temperature with bowls of steamed rice.

Serves 4

takoyaki

batter
150 g (5½ oz/1 cup) plain (all-purpose)
    flour
1 tablespoon dashi granules
1 egg, lightly beaten
310 ml (10¾ oz/1¼ cups) iced water

oil, for frying
50 g (1¾ oz) octopus tentacle, cut into
    12 pieces
1 spring onion (scallion), thinly sliced
2 tablespoons thinly sliced pickled
    ginger
Japanese mayonnaise, to serve
2 tablespoons bonito flakes, to serve

To make the batter, combine the flour and dashi granules in a bowl. Add the egg and iced water and whisk to make a smooth batter. Set aside.

Generously brush the 12 holes in a takoyaki pan with the oil and place over high heat. When smoking hot, pour the batter into the holes, making sure it reaches almost all the way to the top of each hole. Cook for 2–3 minutes, or until the batter is starting to set around the edges.

Put a piece of octopus in the centre of each hole. Sprinkle over the spring onion and 1 tablespoon of the ginger and continue cooking for 2–3 minutes, or until the batter looks firm around the edges. Use a fork to run around the edge of each hole and remove any stuck on bits of batter. Turn each ball ninety degrees, revealing half the spherical side of each ball. Cook for 2 minutes, then turn over completely so the spherical side of each ball is facing upwards (they should be cooked golden). Cook for a further 2–3 minutes, or until the underside is also golden.

Transfer from the pan to a serving plate. Squeeze a dollop of mayonnaise onto each octopus ball and sprinkle over the remaining ginger and the bonito flakes to serve.

Makes 12

spring onion and cabbage okonomiyaki

75 g (2½ oz/½ cup) plain (all-purpose) flour
1 tablespoon dashi granules
1 egg, lightly beaten
120 g (4¼ oz/1 cup) thinly sliced spring onions (scallions)
90 g (3¼ oz/2 cups) finely chopped Chinese cabbage

60 ml (2 fl oz/¼ cup) oil
Japanese mayonnaise, to serve
tonkatsu sauce, to serve
2 tablespoons bonito flakes, to serve
1 tablespoon nori flakes, to serve

Combine the flour and dashi granules in a bowl. Add the egg and 250 ml (9 fl oz/1 cup) water and whisk until the mixture is lump free. Stir through the spring onions and cabbage.

Heat the oil in a non-stick frying pan over medium heat until the surface of the oil is shimmering. Pour in the spring onion mixture and use a spatula or large spoon to roughly shape it into a circle about 15 cm (6 in) in diameter. Cook for 5 minutes, then turn over and cook for another 5 minutes, or until golden on both sides.

To serve, squeeze the mayonnaise from the container to make several lines across the top of the okonomiyaki. Repeat with the tonkatsu sauce, then sprinkle with the bonito and nori flakes.

Makes 1

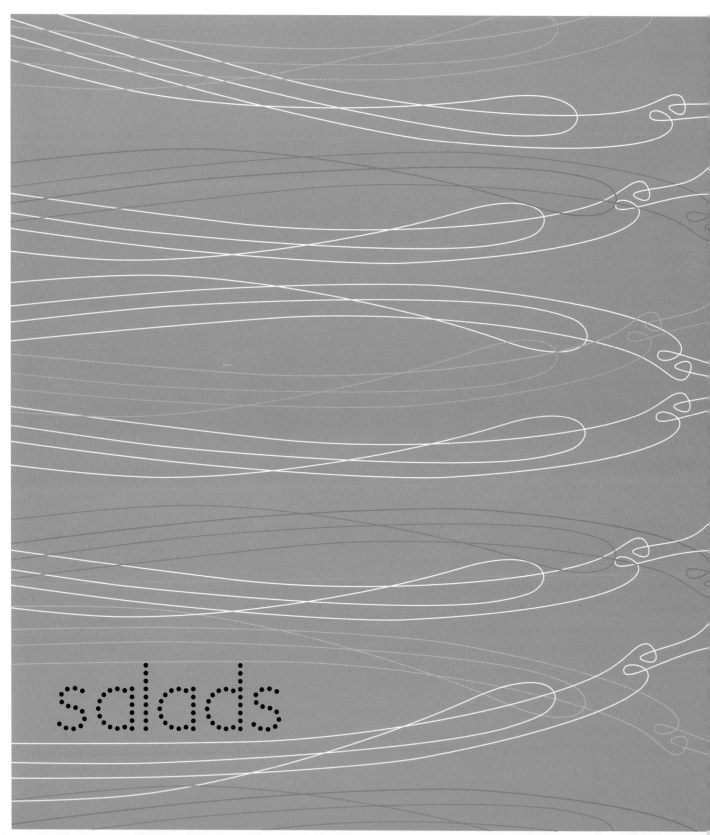

salads

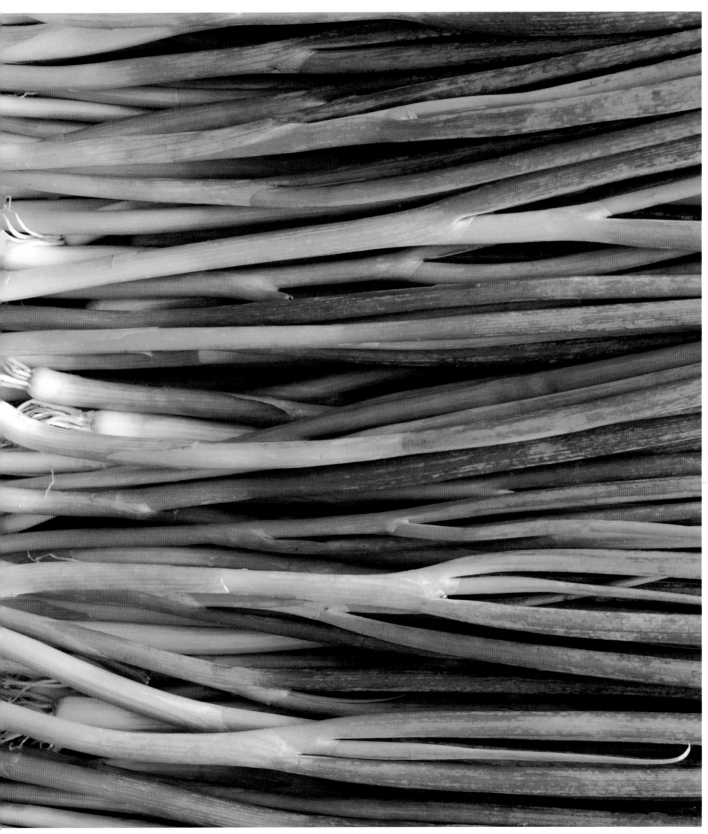

japanese-style potato salad

dressing
175 g (6 oz/¾ cup) Japanese
    mayonnaise
¼ teaspoon sesame oil
½ teaspoon mustard powder
2 tablespoons Japanese rice
    vinegar
3 spring onions (scallions),
    finely chopped
3 tablespoons finely chopped
    flat-leaf parsley
salt and freshly ground
    black pepper

750 g (1 lb 10 oz) boiling
    potatoes, such as dutch
    cream or sebago
75 g (2¾ oz) sliced leg ham

To make the dressing, combine the mayonnaise, sesame oil, mustard powder and vinegar in a bowl. Stir through the spring onion and parsley and season to taste.

Peel the potatoes and cut into 2 cm (¾ in) pieces. Put the potatoes in a saucepan and cover with cold water. Bring to the boil over high heat. Reduce the heat to low, cover with a tight fitting lid and cook for 20 minutes, or until tender.

Drain the potatoes and rinse under cold water until completely cool. Put into a large bowl with the ham, pour over the dressing and gently toss to combine.

Serves 4

green salad with creamy dressing

dressing

3 tablespoons Japanese
  mayonnaise
1 tablespoon lemon juice
¼ teaspoon Japanese mustard
  or 1 teaspoon hot English
  mustard
1 teaspoon Japanese soy
  sauce
5 drops of sesame oil

120 g (4¼ oz/3 cups) mizuna
  or rocket (arugula) leaves
1 avocado, sliced

To make the dressing, combine all the ingredients in a small bowl.
Set aside for 1 hour to allow the flavours to develop.

Combine the mizuna or rocket and avocado in a bowl. Add the
dressing, toss gently to coat and serve on a large platter.

Serves 4

daikon and wakame salad

dressing
2 teaspoons Japanese rice
  vinegar
2 teaspoons Japanese soy sauce
1 teaspoon mirin
½ teaspoon caster (superfine)
  sugar

1 tablespoon dried shredded
  wakame
1 small ripe pear, peeled, cored
  and julienned
50 g (1¾ oz) daikon, julienned
40 g (1½ oz/1 cup) mizuna
  leaves

To make the dressing, combine all the ingredients in a jug with
1 teaspoon of water.

Soak the wakame in a bowl of cold water for 5 minutes, or until soft.
Drain well and thinly slice.

Combine the wakame, pear, daikon and mizuna in a serving bowl.
Add the dressing and toss to coat.

Serves 4

crab and wakame salad

dressing
2 tablespoons Japanese
  soy sauce
1 tablespoon Japanese rice
  vinegar
2 teaspoons dashi granules
2 teaspoons mirin

3 tablespoons dried shredded
  wakame
2 Lebanese (short) cucumbers
2 teaspoons salt
200 g (7 oz) fresh crabmeat
1 teaspoon toasted sesame seeds
pinch of dried chilli flakes
lemon wedges, to serve

To make the dressing, combine all the ingredients in a small saucepan. Cook, stirring, over medium heat until the dashi granules have dissolved. Remove from the heat and set aside to cool.

Soak the wakame in a bowl of cold water for 5 minutes, or until soft. Drain well and set aside.

Cut the cucumbers in half lengthways and use a teaspoon to scoop out the seeds. Thinly slice the cucumber into half moons and put in a bowl with the salt and 500 ml (17 fl oz/2 cups) water. Stir well to dissolve the salt. Leave for 10 minutes, then drain well and squeeze out as much water as possible from the cucumber.

Combine the wakame, cucumber, crabmeat and dressing in a bowl and toss gently. Sprinkle over the sesame seeds and chilli flakes and serve with the lemon wedges on the side.

Serves 4

soba noodle salad

dipping sauce
3 tablespoons dashi granules
125 ml (4 fl oz/½ cup) Japanese
    soy sauce
80 ml (2½ fl oz/⅓ cup) mirin

50 g (9 oz) soba (buckwheat)
    noodles
1 small red or orange carrot,
    julienned
275 g (2½ oz) daikon, julienned
4 spring onions (scallions),
    green part only, thinly sliced
finely shredded nori, to garnish
pickled ginger, to serve
wasabi, optional, to serve

To make the dipping sauce, combine all the ingredients in a small saucepan with 250 ml (9 fl oz/1 cup) cold water and place over medium heat. Bring to the boil, then remove from the heat and set aside to cool.

Bring a large saucepan of water to the boil. Add the noodles and stir to separate. Add 250 ml (9 fl oz/1 cup) cold water to the pan and return to the boil. Repeat this process twice more, or until the noodles are cooked evenly. Rinse under cold water, using your hands to separate, until the noodles are cool. Drain well and set aside.

Bring a small saucepan of water to the boil. Add the carrot and daikon and cook for 30 seconds, or until just tender. Drain, then put the vegetables in a bowl of iced water until chilled. Drain well.

Combine the noodles with the carrot, daikon and spring onion. Scatter over the nori and serve with the dipping sauce, ginger and wasabi, if desired.

Serves 4

green beans with black sesame dressing

dressing
40 g (1½ oz/¼ cup) black
   sesame seeds
1 teaspoon sugar
2 tablespoons white miso
2 tablespoons mirin

300 g (10½ oz) green beans,
   trimmed and cut into
   4 cm (1½ in) lengths
toasted sesame seeds, optional,
   to garnish

To make the dressing, put the sesame seeds in a non-stick frying pan. Cook over medium heat, shaking the pan, until the seeds just start to smoke and become aromatic. Remove from the pan and allow to cool. Pour the seeds into a suribachi or mortar and pound until finely crushed. Add the sugar, miso and mirin and stir to make a paste.

Bring a large saucepan of water to the boil. Add the beans and cook for 2 minutes, or until just tender. Drain, then put the beans into a bowl of ice water until completely cool.

Drain the beans well and combine in a bowl with the dressing. Sprinkle over the toasted sesame seeds, if desired.

Serves 4

lotus root salad

dressing
3 tablespoons Japanese
    mayonnaise
1 teaspoon Japanese rice vinegar

dash of Japanese rice vinegar
120 g (4¼ oz) lotus root,
    peeled and thinly sliced
½ carrot, julienned
handful of snow pea (mangetout)
    sprouts
salmon roe, to serve

To make the dressing, combine the mayonnaise and vinegar in a small bowl.

Bring a saucepan of water to the boil. Add the vinegar and lotus root. Cook for 1 minute, or until tender. Drain and rinse under cold water.

Combine the lotus root, carrot and sprouts in a bowl. Add the dressing and toss to combine. Top with some salmon roe to serve.

Serves 4

cabbage salad with sesame dressing

dressing
1½ tablespoons toasted sesame
    seeds
1 teaspoon Japanese rice vinegar
1 tablespoon Japanese soy sauce
1 teaspoon mirin
1 teaspoon sugar

80 g (2¾ oz/1 cup) finely
    shredded red cabbage
80 g (2¾ oz/1 cup) finely
    shredded green cabbage

To make the dressing, put the sesame seeds and rice vinegar in a suribachi or mortar and pound to a paste. Add the remaining ingredients and stir to combine.

Combine the cabbages and dressing in a bowl and transfer to a large bowl to serve.

Serves 4

soft-shell crab salad with ponzu

ponzu sauce
60 ml (2 fl oz/¼ cup) Japanese
　　soy sauce
1 tablespoon lemon juice
1 tablespoon lime juice
1 tablespoon Japanese
　　rice vinegar
1 tablespoon mirin
½ teaspoon sugar
1 tablespoon bonito flakes

1 tablespoon sea salt
125 g (4½ oz/1 cup) cornflour
　　(cornstarch)
500 g (1 lb 2 oz) soft-shell crab
3 egg whites, lightly beaten
1 litre (35 fl oz/4 cups) canola oil
1 cup shiso leaves
2 spring onions (scallions), green
　　part only, thinly sliced
ichimi powder, to serve
lemon wedges, to serve

To make the ponzu sauce, combine all the ingredients in a bowl and chill until needed.

Combine the salt and cornflour in a bowl. Cut the crabs in half. Dip each piece of crab into the egg white, then into the cornflour to evenly coat all over.

Heat the oil in a wok or large saucepan over high heat. The oil is ready when the surface is shimmering. Add half of the crab pieces and cook for 2–3 minutes, or until golden. Drain on paper towel. Repeat for the remaining crab.

Put the crab pieces in a large bowl with the shiso leaves and spring onion. Add the dressing and toss to combine. Serve with the ichimi powder and lemon wedges on the side.

Serves 4

green tea noodle salad

dressing
80 ml (2½ fl oz/⅓ cup) Japanese soy
    sauce
2 tablespoons Japanese rice vinegar
1 tablespoon sesame oil
1 teaspoon sugar

125 ml (4 fl oz/½ cup) oil
4 won ton wrappers
3 tablespoons dried shredded wakame
250 g (9 oz) green tea noodles
8 cherry tomatoes, halved
4 spring onions (scallions), green part
    only, thinly sliced

To make the dressing, combine all the ingredients in a bowl and set aside.

Heat the oil in a small frying pan over high heat. When the surface of the oil is shimmering, add two won ton wrappers and cook for 1 minute. Turn over and cook for another minute, or until golden. Drain on paper towel. Repeat this process to cook the remaining won ton wrappers. Allow to cool, then roughly break the won tons into 1 cm (½ in) pieces and set aside.

Soak the wakame in a bowl of cold water for 5 minutes, or until soft. Drain well and set aside.

Bring a large saucepan of water to the boil. Add the noodles and stir to separate. Add 250 ml (9 fl oz/1 cup) cold water to the saucepan and return to the boil. Repeat this process twice more, or until the noodles are cooked evenly. Rinse under cold water, using your hands to separate, until the noodles are cool. Drain well.

Place the noodles, dressing, wakame, tomatoes and spring onion in a large bowl and toss to combine. Add the crispy won ton pieces, toss again and serve.

Serves 4

edamame salad with miso dressing

miso dressing
2 tablespoons white miso
1 teaspoon Japanese rice vinegar
1 teaspoon mirin
½ teaspoon caster (superfine)
    sugar
¼ teaspoon Japanese mustard

200 g (7 oz) frozen edamame
    beans, in the pod
handful of mizuna or rocket
    (arugula) leaves

To make the miso dressing, combine all the ingredients in a small bowl with 1 tablespoon of warm water. Set aside for 1 hour to allow the flavours to develop.

Half fill a wok or large saucepan with water and bring to the boil. Put the edamame in a bamboo steamer and sit it over the top of the wok or saucepan. Cover tightly and steam for 5 minutes, or until tender. Allow to cool slightly, then remove the beans from the pods.

Combine the edamame and mizuna or rocket in a large bowl and drizzle with the miso dressing to serve.

Serves 4

skewers

tofu and vegetable skewers

100 g (3½ oz) firm tofu, cut into
    2 cm (¾ in) cubes
1 red capsicum (pepper), cut
    into 2 cm (¾ in) pieces
4 asparagus spears, cut into
    2 cm (¾ in) lengths
8 bamboo skewers, soaked in
    water for 30 minutes
1 tablespoon oil
ichimi powder, to serve

soy and mirin sauce
60 ml (2 fl oz/¼ cup)
    Japanese soy sauce
2 tablespoons mirin
2 tablespoons sake
1 tablespoon sugar
2 teaspoons cornflour
    (cornstarch)

Thread alternating pieces of tofu, capsicum and asparagus onto the skewers, making sure that the skewers have a similar amount of each ingredient.

Heat a chargrill pan or barbecue hotplate to high and brush with the oil. Cook the skewers for 8 minutes, turning every couple of minutes, until the tofu and vegetables are golden.

While the skewers are cooking, combine the sauce ingredients in a small saucepan and cook, stirring, over high heat for 2–3 minutes, or until thickened.

Brush the sauce over the skewers and sprinkle over some ichimi powder to serve.

Makes 8

grilled squid with soy and mirin

60 ml (2 fl oz/¼ cup) Japanese
    soy sauce
60 ml (2 fl oz/¼ cup) mirin
1 tablespoon sugar
300 g (10½ oz) squid tubes, cut
    into 5 mm (¼ in) thick rings

4 bamboo skewers, soaked
    in water for 30 minutes
1 tablespoon oil
ichimi powder, to serve
lemon wedges, to serve

Combine the soy sauce, mirin and sugar in a small bowl. Add the squid and place in the fridge to marinate for at least 30 minutes.

Drain the squid from the marinade and thread three squid rings onto each skewer.

Heat a chargrill pan or barbecue hotplate to high and brush with the oil. Cook the skewers for 2 minutes on each side, or until pale golden.

Sprinkle with the ichimi powder and serve with the lemon wedges on the side.

Makes 4

chicken and shiitake skewers

....

2 tablespoons Japanese soy
    sauce
2 tablespoons mirin
2 tablespoons Japanese rice
    vinegar
½ teaspoon Japanese chilli oil
400 g (14 oz) boneless, skinless
    chicken breast, cut into 3 cm
    (1¼ in) pieces

4 bamboo skewers, soaked in
    water for 30 minutes
2 spring onions (scallions), cut
    into 4 cm (1½ in) lengths
8 small shiitake mushrooms,
    stems removed
1 tablespoon oil

Combine the soy sauce, mirin, vinegar and chilli oil in a bowl. Add the chicken, stir to combine and place in the fridge to marinate for 3–6 hours, stirring often.

Remove the chicken from the marinade and thread onto the skewers, alternating with the spring onion and mushrooms, so that each skewer has similar quantities of each.

Preheat the griller (broiler) to high. Brush the skewers with the oil and grill for about 8 minutes, turning every 2 minutes, until golden.

Makes 4

marinated tofu skewers

300 g (10½ oz) silken firm tofu
potato flour, to dust
2 tablespoons oil
4 bamboo skewers, soaked in
    water for 30 minutes
steamed rice, to serve

marinade
60 ml (2 fl oz/¼ cup) Japanese
    soy sauce
2 tablespoons sake
2 tablespoons mirin
1 teaspoon finely grated ginger
2 spring onions (scallions),
    finely chopped, green
    part reserved for garnish

Place the tofu on a plate. Top with another plate and set aside, occasionally draining the liquid that escapes, for 2 hours. Cut into eight pieces.

To make the marinade, combine all the ingredients. Transfer half to a small serving bowl. Place the tofu in the remaining marinade and leave to marinate for 20 minutes. Drain and pat dry.

Place some potato flour on a plate. Add the tofu and toss to coat.

Heat the oil in a large frying pan over medium–high heat. Add the tofu and cook, turning carefully, for 3 minutes, or until crisp.

Thread two pieces of tofu onto each skewer. Sprinkle with the reserved spring onion and serve with the rice and the reserved marinade for dipping.

Makes 4

chilli prawns

1 tablespoon sake
1 teaspoon Japanese chilli paste
1 teaspoon caster (superfine)
    sugar
8 raw prawns (shrimp), peeled,
    deveined and tails intact

8 bamboo skewers, soaked
    in water for 30 minutes
1 tablespoon oil
lime cheeks, to serve

Combine the sake, chilli paste and sugar in a small bowl.

Use a small, sharp knife to make three small incisions on the underside of the prawns (this will prevent them from curling as they cook). Add the prawns to the sake mixture and toss to combine. Cover with plastic wrap and place in the fridge to marinate for at least 4 hours.

Thread each prawn lengthways onto a skewer, starting at the tail.

Heat a chargrill pan or barbecue hotplate to high and brush with the oil. Add the prawns and cook, basting with the marinade, for 1–2 minutes on each side, or until golden and cooked. Serve with the lime cheeks.

Makes 8

spring onion skewers

60 ml (2 fl oz/¼ cup) Japanese
   soy sauce
2 tablespoons mirin
2 tablespoons sake
1 tablespoon sugar

8 spring onions (scallions), cut
   into 4 cm (1½ in) lengths
8 bamboo skewers, soaked
   in water for 30 minutes
1 tablespoon oil

Combine the soy sauce, mirin, sake and sugar in a small bowl and set aside.

Bring a saucepan of water to the boil. Add the spring onion and cook for 1 minute, or until just tender. Drain and quickly put the spring onion into a bowl of cold water until cool. Drain well, then thread four spring onion pieces onto each skewer.

Preheat a chargrill pan or barbecue hotplate to high and brush with the oil. Cook the skewers for 2–3 minutes on each side, or until the spring onions are golden and softened.

Brush the soy mixture over the spring onion and cook for another minute on each side, or until golden.

Makes 8

grilled scallops with nori

60 ml (2 fl oz/¼ cup) ponzu sauce
  (page 66)
2 tablespoons mirin
2 teaspoons caster (superfine)
  sugar
2 teaspoons sesame oil
16 scallops, roe attached

2 teaspoons nori flakes
2 teaspoons toasted sesame
  seeds
8 bamboo skewers, soaked
  in water for 30 minutes
1 tablespoon oil
lime wedges, to serve

Combine the ponzu, mirin, sugar and sesame oil in a bowl. Add the scallops and place in the fridge to marinate for 30 minutes.

Strain the marinade into a small saucepan and cook over medium heat for 4–5 minutes, or until thickened. Set aside.

Combine the nori flakes and sesame seeds in a small bowl.

Thread two scallops onto each skewer and sprinkle the nori and sesame mix over the scallops.

Heat a chargrill pan or barbecue hotplate to high and brush with the oil. Cook the scallops for about 2 minutes on each side, or until lightly golden. Serve with the lime wedges on the side.

Makes 8

prosciutto and asparagus skewers

glaze
1 tablespoon Japanese soy sauce
½ teaspoon sesame oil
½ teaspoon caster (superfine)
   sugar
1 small garlic clove, finely
   chopped

8 asparagus spears, woody
   ends trimmed
4 thin slices prosciutto, cut
   in half widthways
8 bamboo skewers, soaked
   in water for 30 minutes
toasted sesame seeds,
   optional, to garnish

To make the glaze, combine all the ingredients in a small bowl.

Bring a deep frying pan of water to a simmer. Add the asparagus and cook for 3 minutes, or until just tender. Rinse well under cold running water. Cut each spear into four lengths.

Wrap a piece of prosciutto around four asparagus lengths. Thread onto a skewer. Repeat with the remaining prosciutto and asparagus.

Preheat a griller (broiler) to high. Put the skewers on a baking tray and brush with the glaze. Grill, brushing occasionally with the glaze, for 3–4 minutes, or until crisp.

Serve sprinkled with the sesame seeds, if desired.

Makes 8

beef and spring onion skewers

....

marinade
2 tablespoons toasted sesame seeds
80 ml (2½ fl oz/⅓ cup) Japanese
    soy sauce
2 tablespoons mirin
1 teaspoon sesame oil
2 teaspoons caster (superfine) sugar
pinch of ichimi powder, optional

350 g (12 oz) rump steak
3 spring onions (scallions), cut into
    5 cm (2 in) lengths
4 bamboo skewers, soaked in water
    for 30 minutes

To make the marinade, place the sesame seeds in a suribachi or mortar and pound until smooth. Transfer to a bowl and stir in the remaining marinade ingredients. Transfer half of the mixture to a small serving bowl.

Use a mallet to beat the steak to a thickness of 3 mm (⅛ in). Cut into 12 strips, each measuring approximately 7 x 3 cm (2¾ x 1¼ in). Add to the marinade and place in the fridge to marinate for 30 minutes.

Drain the beef and pat dry. Place a length of spring onion across the short end of a piece of beef. Roll to enclose. Repeat with the remaining beef and spring onion. Thread three pieces of beef onto each skewer.

Preheat a chargrill pan or barbecue hotplate to medium–high. Cook the skewers for about 2–3 minutes on each side, or until cooked to your liking.

Serve with the reserved marinade for dipping.

Makes 4

chicken skewers with sake and soy

marinade
2 tablespoons sake
2 tablespoons Japanese soy sauce
2 tablespoons mirin
1½ tablespoons lemon juice
1 spring onion (scallion), thinly
  sliced

4 boneless, skinless chicken
  thighs
12 bamboo skewers, soaked in
  water for 30 minutes
finely sliced spring onion
  (scallion), to serve
steamed rice, to serve

Combine the marinade ingredients in a shallow dish. Add the chicken and set aside to marinate for 30 minutes.

Remove the chicken, reserving the marinade, and pat dry with paper towel. Insert three skewers into each fillet.

Preheat the griller (broiler) to medium–high. Place the skewers on a baking tray. Grill, basting occasionally with the reserved marinade and turning, for 12 minutes, or until cooked through.

Scatter with the spring onion and serve with the rice.

Makes 4

shiitake and sesame skewers

60 ml (2 fl oz/¼ cup) Japanese
   soy sauce
2 teaspoons caster (superfine)
   sugar
½ teaspoon sesame oil
8 large shiitake mushrooms,
   stems removed

4 bamboo skewers, soaked in
   water for 30 minutes
1 tablespoon oil
1 spring onion (scallion), finely
   sliced, to serve

Combine the soy sauce, sugar and sesame oil in a bowl. Add the mushrooms and set aside to marinate for 3 hours.

Thread two mushrooms onto each skewer.

Heat a chargrill pan or barbecue hotplate to high and brush with the oil. Cook the skewers for 2–3 minutes on each side, or until the mushrooms have softened and are browned around the edges.

Scatter on the spring onion and serve.

Makes 4

pork skewers with umeboshi

600 g (1 lb 5 oz) pork fillet, cut into 2 cm
   (¾ in) cubes
1 tablespoon Japanese soy sauce
1 teaspoon sesame oil
8 bamboo skewers, soaked in water for
   30 minutes
1 tablespoon oil
1 spring onion (scallion), green part only,
   thinly sliced into strips, to serve

umeboshi sauce
2 teaspoons umeboshi (pickled plum)
   paste
60 ml (2 fl oz/¼ cup) Japanese soy
   sauce
2 tablespoons mirin
2 tablespoons sake
1 tablespoon caster (superfine) sugar
1 teaspoon cornflour (cornstarch)

Combine the pork, soy sauce and sesame oil in a bowl. Set aside to marinate for 30 minutes.

Thread the pork onto the skewers, making sure each skewer has a similar amount of meat.

Heat a chargrill pan or barbecue hotplate to high and brush with the oil. Cook the skewers for 8–10 minutes, turning every 2–3 minutes, until the pork is golden brown.

While the skewers are cooking, combine the umeboshi sauce ingredients in a small saucepan and place over high heat. Bring to the boil, stirring, and cook for 4–5 minutes, or until thickened and glazed.

Brush the sauce over the skewers, sprinkle with the spring onion and serve.

Makes 8

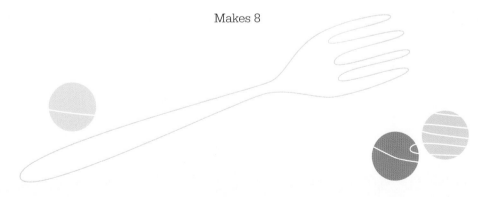

duck with umeboshi

2 tablespoons umeboshi (pickled plum) paste
2 tablespoons sake
1 tablespoon caster (superfine) sugar
220 g (7¾ oz) boneless duck breast, cut into 3 cm (1¼ in) pieces

4 bamboo skewers, soaked in water for 30 minutes
1 spring onion (scallion), green part only, thinly sliced on the diagonal

Combine the umeboshi paste, sake and sugar in a bowl. Add the duck and stir to coat. Cover with plastic wrap and place in the fridge to marinate for 2 hours.

Preheat the griller (broiler) to medium–high. Thread the duck onto the skewers, reserving the marinade.

Place the duck flesh-side up on a baking tray and grill for 4 minutes. Turn and brush with the reserved marinade, then grill for a further 4 minutes, or until the skin is crisp.

Transfer to a serving plate and scatter with the spring onion to serve.

Makes 4

beef teriyaki

teriyaki sauce
60 ml (2 fl oz/¼ cup) Japanese
  soy sauce
2 tablespoons mirin
2 tablespoons sake
1 tablespoon sugar

500 g (1 lb 2 oz) rump steak
1 teaspoon cornflour
  (cornstarch)
12 bamboo skewers, soaked
  in water for 30 minutes
1 tablespoon oil
sesame seeds, to serve

To make the teriyaki sauce, combine all the ingredients in a bowl.

Finely slice the beef into strips, cutting across the grain. Add to the teriyaki sauce and stir to evenly coat the beef. Cover and place in the fridge to marinate for 3 hours.

Strain the sauce into a small saucepan. Add the cornflour and stir to combine. Cook the sauce over medium heat for 2 minutes, or until thickened and no longer cloudy. Set aside.

Thread the beef onto the skewers so that each skewer has the same amount of meat.

Heat a chargrill pan or barbecue hotplate to high and brush with the oil. Cook the skewers for 4–5 minutes, turning every minute or so, until the meat is browned.

Brush the skewers evenly with the teriyaki sauce, sprinkle on the sesame seeds and serve.

Makes 12

fish cake skewers

2 dried shiitake mushrooms
2 teaspoons potato flour
250 g (9 oz) firm white fish fillet,
    roughly chopped
1 tablespoon Japanese soy sauce
2 teaspoons sake
2 teaspoons caster (superfine)
    sugar
pinch of salt
80 g (2¾ oz/½ cup) grated carrot

2 spring onions (scallions),
    thinly sliced
2 tablespoons finely chopped
    shiso leaves, optional
6 bamboo skewers, soaked in
    water for 30 minutes
2 tablespoons oil
finely grated daikon, to serve
lemon cheeks, to serve

Put the mushrooms in a heatproof bowl and cover with boiling water. Set aside for 30 minutes to soak. Drain. Remove the woody stems, then thinly slice the mushrooms.

Combine the flour and 2 teaspoons of water in a small bowl. Place the fish, flour mixture, soy sauce, sake, sugar and salt in the bowl of a food processor. Process to a paste.

Transfer the paste to a bowl and add the shiitake, carrot, spring onion and shiso (if using). Stir to combine. Divide the mixture into six portions and shape each one around a skewer (there should be about 2 tablespoons in each portion).

Heat the oil in a large frying pan over medium–high heat. Add the skewers and cook, turning occasionally, for 5–7 minutes, or until cooked through.

Serve with the grated daikon and lemon cheeks.

Makes 6

chicken balls

1 teaspoon Japanese soy sauce
1 teaspoon sake
1 teaspoon mirin
1 teaspoon grated ginger
2 teaspoons cornflour (cornstarch)
230 g (8 oz) minced (ground)
    chicken
4 bamboo skewers, soaked in
    water for 30 minutes
1 teaspoon oil

glaze
1 tablespoon Japanese soy
    sauce
1 teaspoon mirin
1 teaspoon caster (superfine)
    sugar

Combine the soy sauce, sake, mirin, ginger and cornflour in a bowl. Add the minced chicken and stir well.

Use wet hands to roll the mixture into 12 balls (about 1 tablespoon of mixture in each). Put the balls on a tray lined with baking paper and place in the fridge for 30 minutes.

Meanwhile, place the glaze ingredients in a small bowl and stir to dissolve the sugar.

Thread three balls onto each skewer. Lightly brush a large frying pan with the oil and place over medium heat. Add the skewers and cook, turning and basting with the glaze, for 8 minutes, or until cooked through.

Makes 4

crisp pork belly skewers

braising liquid
250 ml (9 fl oz/1 cup) dashi stock
80 ml (2½ fl oz/⅓ cup) sake
60 ml (2 fl oz/¼ cup) Japanese soy sauce
2 tablespoons mirin
2 tablespoons caster (superfine) sugar
3 thin slices fresh ginger

350 g (12 oz) boneless pork, rind
    removed and cut into 8 pieces
8 bamboo skewers, soaked in water
    for 30 minutes
½ spring onion (scallion), thinly sliced
½ long red chilli, seeded and thinly
    sliced
1 teaspoon oil
3–4 drops of toasted sesame oil

To make the braising liquid, combine all the ingredients in a saucepan over medium–high heat. Stir to dissolve the sugar.

Add the pork to the braising liquid and bring to the boil. Reduce the heat to low and partially cover with a lid. Simmer, checking often to ensure the sauce does not burn, for 1 hour and 15 minutes, or until the pork is tender. Use a slotted spoon to transfer the pork to a plate.

Preheat the griller (broiler) to medium–high. Thread a piece of pork onto each skewer, put on a baking tray and brush with the braising liquid. Grill for 2–3 minutes on each side, or until crisp and golden.

Combine the spring onion, chilli, oil and sesame oil in a bowl. Transfer the skewers to a serving plate and sprinkle with the spring onion mixture to serve.

Makes 8

miso-glazed salmon skewers

glaze
3 tablespoons white miso
3 teaspoons caster (superfine)
    sugar
3 teaspoons sake
3 teaspoons mirin

320 g (11¼ oz) salmon fillet,
    cut into 8 pieces, each
    8 x 2 cm (3¼ x ¾ in)
8 bamboo skewers, soaked
    in water for 30 minutes
lemon wedges, to serve

To make the glaze, combine all the ingredients in a bowl. Add the salmon and toss to coat. Cover with plastic wrap and place in the fridge for 30 minutes to marinate.

Thread a piece of salmon onto each skewer.

Preheat the griller (broiler) to high and line a baking tray with baking paper.

Put the skewers on the tray and grill, turning and brushing with the glaze, for 5 minutes, or until cooked to your liking. Transfer to a plate and serve with the lemon wedges.

Makes 8

sharing plates

pork and cabbage gyoza

dipping sauce
1 tablespoon Japanese rice vinegar
1 tablespoon Japanese soy sauce
few drops of chilli oil
½ spring onion (scallion), thinly sliced

250 g (9 oz) minced (ground) pork
25 g (1 oz/½ cup) finely shredded
    Chinese cabbage
2 tablespoons Japanese soy sauce
2 teaspoons finely grated ginger
1 teaspoon sesame oil
pinch of salt
pinch of white pepper
28 gow gee or gyoza wrappers
1 tablespoon oil

To make the dipping sauce, combine all the ingredients in a small bowl.

Put the minced pork, cabbage, soy sauce, ginger, sesame oil, salt and pepper in a bowl and mix well.

Sit a gow gee wrapper in the palm of your hand. Place 2 teaspoons of the pork mixture in the centre of the wrapper. Use a finger to rub water around the edge of the wrapper and press the sides together to seal. Rub a little more water along the rim of the seam and pleat together. Gently tap the bottom of the gyoza on a work surface to flatten. Repeat this process with the remaining wrappers and pork mixture.

Heat half of the oil in a large frying pan over high heat. Add half of the gyoza and reduce the heat to medium–high. Cook the gyoza for 2 minutes, without moving them, or until the bases are golden. Add 125 ml (4½ fl oz/½ cup) water and simmer for 5 minutes, or until the gyoza are cooked and the water evaporated. Transfer to a serving plate and cover with foil to keep warm. Repeat with the remaining oil, gyoza and another 125 ml (4½ fl oz/½ cup) water.

Serve immediately with the dipping sauce.

Makes 28

onigiri with umeboshi and tofu

440 g (15½ oz/2 cups) Japanese
   short-grain rice
3 teaspoons umeboshi (pickled plum)
   paste
100 g (3½ oz) silken tofu, mashed

1 tablespoon finely chopped shiso
   leaves
1 teaspoon sesame oil
6 whole shiso leaves
2 tablespoons toasted sesame seeds

Wash the rice in a sieve under cold running water. Put the rice and 685 ml (23½ fl oz/2¾ cups) cold water in a small, heavy-based saucepan and bring to the boil over high heat. Cover with a tight fitting lid, reduce the heat to low and cook for 15 minutes. Remove from the heat, fluff the rice with a spatula or large spoon and cover with a clean tea towel. Set aside for 15 minutes.

Combine the umeboshi paste, tofu and shiso in a bowl.

Line a teacup with plastic wrap, making sure it hangs over the side. Brush the plastic wrap with water. Gently press 1 loosely packed cup of rice into the teacup. Use a finger to make an indentation in the centre of the rice and put 2 teaspoons of the tofu mixture into the indentation. Draw the sides of the plastic wrap over the rice, remove from the teacup and firmly twist to enclose the rice. Keep twisting until the rice forms a ball. Repeat this process to make another five rice balls (avoid using any hardened rice on the base of the saucepan). Leave the rice wrapped in the plastic and set aside for 30 minutes.

Preheat the griller (broiler) to high and line a baking tray with baking paper.

Unwrap the rice balls and lightly brush with the sesame oil. Place on the baking tray and grill, turning often, for about 2–3 minutes, or until the rice is just turning golden

To serve, place each onigiri on a shiso leaf and sprinkle with the sesame seeds.

Makes 6

eggplant with miso

4 tablespoons red miso
1 tablespoon mirin
2 teaspoons caster (superfine)
   sugar

6 Japanese eggplants
   (aubergines)
1 tablespoon oil
1 teaspoon toasted sesame
   seeds

Combine the miso, mirin and sugar in a small bowl. Add
2 tablespoons of boiling water and stir until smooth. Set aside.

Preheat the griller (broiler) to high and line a baking tray with
baking paper.

Cut each eggplant in half lengthways. Brush all over with the oil and
lay cut-side down on the prepared tray.

Grill the eggplant for 2–3 minutes, or until the skin has softened and
is beginning to darken. Turn over and grill for another 2 minutes, or
until the flesh is golden but not burning.

Brush the miso mixture over the cut side of the eggplant and grill
for another 2–3 minutes, or until the miso mixture is just bubbling
(be careful not to let it burn).

Sprinkle over the sesame seeds to serve.

Serves 4

agedashi tofu

....

300 g (10½ oz) silken firm tofu
250 ml (9 fl oz/1 cup) dashi stock
2 tablespoons mirin
2 tablespoons Japanese soy sauce
1 teaspoon caster (superfine)
    sugar
1 teaspoon finely grated ginger

oil, for frying
potato flour, for dusting
1 spring onion (scallion), thinly
    sliced
1 tablespoon thinly sliced nori
1 tablespoon bonito flakes

Put the tofu on a plate and top with another plate. Set aside, occasionally draining the liquid that escapes, for 2 hours. Cut into four pieces.

Combine the dashi stock, mirin, soy sauce, sugar and ginger in a saucepan and place over medium heat. Cook, stirring, for 3 minutes, or until the sugar dissolves.

Pour enough oil into a wok or deep frying pan to come 5 cm (2 in) up the side. Lightly dust the tofu in potato flour. Cook the tofu, turning, for 3 minutes, or until lightly golden and crisp.

Drain the tofu on paper towel and transfer to a bowl. Pour over the dashi mixture. Scatter over the spring onion, nori and bonito flakes and serve immediately.

Serves 4

potato croquettes

450 g (1 lb) all-purpose potatoes,
    peeled and roughly chopped
salt
4 spring onions (scallions), thinly
    sliced
white pepper
2 tablespoons plain
    (all-purpose) flour

1 egg, lightly beaten
60 g (2¼ oz/1 cup) panko
    (Japanese breadcrumbs)
oil, for frying
lemon wedges, to serve
mizuna or rocket (arugula)
    leaves, to serve

Bring a saucepan of lightly salted water to the boil. Add the potato and cook for 20 minutes, or until tender. Drain and use a potato masher to mash until smooth. Stir through the spring onion and season with salt and pepper. Set aside until cool enough to handle.

Divide the mixture into four even portions and mould the portions into patties, about 7–8 cm (2¾–3¼ in) in diameter.

Put the flour, egg and panko in separate bowls. Dust the patties with the flour, dip in the egg, then coat with the panko.

Pour enough oil into a deep frying pan to reach 5 cm (2 in) up the side of the pan and place over medium–high heat. Add the croquettes and cook for 1 minute on each side, or until golden.

Drain on paper towel and serve with the lemon wedges and mizuna or rocket leaves.

Makes 4

steamed savoury custards

4 gingko nuts
½ teaspoon dashi granules
3 eggs
1 tablespoon Japanese soy sauce
1 tablespoon sake
pinch of salt

4 raw prawns (shrimp), peeled,
   deveined and cut in half lengthways
2 shiitake mushrooms, stems removed
   and cut in half
4 x 5 mm (¼ in) thick slices kamaboko
   (fish cake)

Put the gingko nuts in a small heatproof bowl. Pour over 250 ml (9 fl oz/1 cup) boiling water. Set aside and leave until the water has cooled. Drain and set aside.

Put the dashi granules in a bowl. Add 125 ml (4 fl oz/½ cup) warm water and stir until the granules have dissolved.

Gently beat the eggs with a pair of chopstick, being careful not to make the eggs go frothy. Add the dashi mixture and 375 ml (13 fl oz/1½ cups) water and stir with chopsticks to combine. Strain through a fine sieve into a bowl. Stir through the soy sauce, sake and salt.

Sit two prawn halves in the base of four 250 ml (9 fl oz/1 cup) ramekins. Top with half a mushroom, a gingko nut and a slice of kamaboko. Gently pour the custard into the cup.

Half fill a wok or large saucepan with water and bring to the boil. Sit a bamboo steamer on top and carefully place the custards inside. Cover tightly and cook for 1 minute. Put a chopstick under the lid of the steamer for the steam to escape. This will ensure the custards cook evenly. Steam for a further 10 minutes, or until a skewer inserted into the centre of a custard comes out clean.

Makes 4

onigiri with salmon and bonito

440 g (15½ oz/2 cups) Japanese
   short-grain rice
125 g (4½ oz) salmon fillet, skin on
½ teaspoon sea salt
3 tablespoons bonito flakes

2 teaspoons Japanese soy sauce
1 tablespoon oil
2 sheets nori
Japanese soy sauce, to serve

Wash the rice in a sieve under cold running water. Put the rice and 685 ml (23½ fl oz/2¾ cups) cold water in a small, heavy-based saucepan and bring to the boil over high heat. Cover with a tight fitting lid, reduce the heat to low and cook for 15 minutes. Remove from the heat, fluff the rice with a spatula or large spoon and cover with a clean tea towel. Set aside for 15 minutes.

Preheat the griller (broiler) to high. Lay the salmon skin-side up on a piece of baking paper and sprinkle the salt on the skin. Grill for 5 minutes, or until the skin is dark golden and puffed. Turn over and cook for another 5 minutes. Remove and allow to cool. When cool enough to handle, peel off the skin, then roughly chop the salmon. Use a fork to finely flake the salmon, then put in a small bowl with the bonito flakes and soy sauce. Mix well.

Line a teacup with plastic wrap, making sure it hangs over the side. Brush the plastic wrap with water. Gently press 1 loosely packed cup of rice into the teacup. Use a finger to make an indentation in the centre of the rice and put 1 tablespoon of the salmon mixture into the indentation. Draw the sides of the plastic wrap over the rice, remove from the teacup and firmly twist to enclose the rice. Keep twisting until the rice forms a ball. Repeat this process to make another five rice balls (avoid using any hardened rice on the base of the saucepan). Leave the rice wrapped in the plastic and set aside for 30 minutes.

Cut the sheets of nori into six 3 cm (1¼ in) wide strips.

Unwrap the rice balls and place one ball in the centre of each piece of nori. Gently press the nori into the sides of the ball and serve with the soy sauce.

Makes 6

scallops with ginger and mirin

dressing
1 tablespoon Japanese soy
   sauce
1 tablespoon mirin
2 teaspoons Japanese rice
   vinegar
1 teaspoon thinly sliced ginger

2 teaspoons dried shredded
   wakame
50 g (1¾ oz) butter, melted
1 teaspoon Japanese soy sauce
¼ teaspoon sesame oil
24 large scallops, on the shell

To make the dressing, combine the soy sauce, mirin, vinegar and ginger in a small bowl.

Soak the wakame in a bowl of cold water for 5 minutes, or until soft. Drain well.

Combine the butter, soy sauce and sesame oil in a small bowl.

Half fill a wok or large saucepan with water and bring to the boil. Arrange the scallops in a large bamboo steamer (if you don't have a large enough steamer, you will need to cook the scallops in batches). Spoon a little of the butter mixture and some wakame onto each scallop.

Sit the steamer over the wok or saucepan, cover tightly and steam for 5 minutes, or until the scallops are cooked.

Serves 6

vegetable gyoza

3 teaspoons Japanese soy sauce
¼ teaspoon caster (superfine) sugar
½ teaspoon cornflour (cornstarch)
2 teaspoons oil
1 garlic clove, finely chopped
2 teaspoons finely grated ginger
1 spring onion (scallion), finely chopped

150 g (5½ oz) finely chopped Chinese
  cabbage
2–3 drops of sesame oil
12 gow gee or gyoza wrappers
3 teaspoons oil, extra
Japanese soy sauce, to serve

Combine the soy sauce, sugar and cornflour in a small bowl and set aside.

Heat the oil in a non-stick frying pan over high heat, swirling the oil around in the pan to coat. Add the garlic, ginger and spring onion and stir-fry for just a few seconds, or until aromatic but not burning. Add the cabbage and stir-fry for 2 minutes, or until the cabbage is very soft. Quickly stir the soy sauce mixture and pour into the frying pan. Stir for 1 minute, or until the cabbage is coated in the sauce. Remove from the heat and allow to cool. Stir through the sesame oil.

Sit a gow gee wrapper in the palm of your hand. Place 2 level teaspoons of the cabbage mixture in the centre of the wrapper. Use a finger to rub water around the edge of the wrapper and press the sides together to seal. Rub a little more water along the rim of the seam and pleat together. Gently tap the bottom of the gyoza on a work surface to flatten. Repeat this process with the remaining wrappers and cabbage mixture.

Heat the extra oil in a heavy-based frying pan over high heat and cook the dumplings for 2 minutes, without moving them. Pour 60 ml (2 fl oz/¼ cup) water into the pan and quickly cover with a lid (be careful as the oil water will splutter on contact with the hot oil). Cook for a further minute, then give the frying pan a few firm shakes to help remove any stuck on bits. Cook for another minute, or until the water has evaporated and the wrappers are cooked.

Serve immediately with the soy sauce.

Makes 12

sake-steamed clams with soy butter

400 g (14 oz) clams (vongole)
60 ml (2 fl oz/¼ cup) sake
2 teaspoons caster (superfine)
    sugar
1 teaspoon Japanese soy sauce

1 teaspoon finely chopped ginger
20 g (¾ oz) unsalted butter,
    chopped and chilled
1 spring onion (scallion), thinly
    sliced

Put the clams in a bowl, cover with cold water and place in the fridge for 2 hours (this helps to release any sand that may be caught in the clams). Drain the clams, rinse under running water and set aside.

Combine the sake, sugar, soy sauce and ginger in a small jug. Stir until the sugar dissolves.

Put the clams in a large frying pan over high heat and add the sake mixture. Cover and cook, shaking the pan occasionally, for 3 minutes, or until the clams open. Use a slotted spoon to transfer the clams to a serving bowl.

Add the chilled butter to the pan juices and whisk until the butter is melted and the sauce is thickened and glossy. Pour the sauce over the clams and sprinkle over the spring onion to serve.

Serves 4

tatsuya fried chicken

marinade
1½ tablespoons Japanese soy sauce
1 tablespoon sake
1 teaspoon grated ginger

250 g (9 oz) boneless, skinless chicken
breast, cut into 4 cm (1½ in) pieces
2 tablespoons Japanese mayonnaise
1 tablespoon finely grated daikon
2 tablespoons plain (all-purpose) flour
2 tablespoons potato flour
2 egg whites, lightly beaten
oil, for frying
steamed rice, to serve

To make the marinade, combine all the ingredients in a bowl. Add the chicken and stir to coat. Cover with plastic wrap and place in the fridge for 2 hours to marinate.

Combine the mayonnaise and daikon in a small bowl. Set aside for 2 hours to allow the flavours to develop.

Drain the chicken from the marinade and pat dry with paper towel. Place the plain flour on a plate. Lightly dust the chicken with the flour. Add the potato flour to the egg white. Place the chicken in the egg white mixture and toss to coat.

Pour enough oil into a wok or deep frying pan to come 5 cm (2 in) up the side and place over medium–high heat until shimmering. Add the chicken and cook for 3–4 minutes on each side, or until golden and cooked through.

Drain on paper towel and serve with the daikon mayonnaise and bowls of rice.

Serves 4

grilled eggplant with soy and ginger

sauce
2 tablespoons Japanese soy sauce
½ teaspoon dashi granules
1 teaspoon mirin
1 teaspoon finely grated ginger
    and its juice

6 Japanese eggplants
    (aubergines)
1 tablespoon oil
bonito flakes, to serve

To make the sauce, combine all the ingredients in a small bowl.
Set aside.

Preheat the griller (broiler) to high and line a baking tray with
baking paper.

Brush the eggplant all over with the oil and put on the baking tray.
Grill for 12–15 minutes, turning every couple of minutes, until the skin
of the eggplant is puffed and blackened. Quickly put the eggplant
into a bowl of chilled water until cool enough to handle.

Peel the eggplant and cut into thirds. Transfer to a bowl and add
the sauce. Toss the eggplant to coat in the sauce and set aside for
30 minutes to allow the flavours to infuse.

Sprinkle over the bonito flakes to serve.

Serves 4

crab croquettes

30 g (1 oz) butter
40 g (1½ oz/½ cup) plain (all-purpose) flour
180 ml (6 fl oz/¾ cup) milk
90 g (3¼ oz/½ cup) fresh crabmeat
125 g (4½ oz) tinned corn kernels, rinsed and drained
1 spring onion (scallion), thinly sliced
salt
white pepper
2 tablespoons plain (all-purpose) flour, extra
1 egg, lightly beaten
60 g (2¼ oz/1 cup) panko (Japanese breadcrumbs)
oil, for frying
mizuna or rocket (arugula) leaves, optional, to serve

Melt the butter in a saucepan over medium–high heat until foamy. Add the flour and cook, stirring, for 2 minutes. Remove the saucepan from the heat and gradually whisk in the milk. Return to the heat and cook, stirring, for about 3–5 minutes, or until very thick. Transfer to a bowl and set aside for 1 hour to cool.

Place the crabmeat and corn on some paper towel and pat with another piece of paper towel to remove excess moisture. Stir the crabmeat, corn and spring onion through the milk mixture and season with the salt and pepper.

Divide the crab mixture into eight portions and mould each one into a log-shaped croquette.

Put the extra flour, egg and panko in separate bowls. Dust the croquettes with the flour, dip in the egg, then coat with the panko.

Pour enough oil into a wok or saucepan to come 5 cm (2 in) up the side and place over medium–high heat until shimmering. Cook the croquettes, in batches, for about 4 minutes, or until golden.

Drain on paper towel and serve with the mizuna or rocket leaves, if desired.

Makes 8

pork okonomiyaki

150 g (5½ oz/1 cup) plain (all-purpose)
  flour
½ teaspoon baking powder
250 ml (9 fl oz/1 cup) dashi stock
1 tablespoon mirin
2 eggs, lightly beaten
40 g (1½ oz/½ cup) finely shredded savoy
  cabbage

2 spring onions (scallions), thinly sliced
1 tablespoon oil
200 g (7 oz) pork fillet, thinly sliced on
  the diagonal
4 tablespoons tonkatsu sauce
4 tablespoons bonito flakes
shredded nori or nori flakes, to serve
Japanese mayonnaise, to serve

Combine the flour and baking powder in a large bowl. Make a well in the centre and, whisking continuously, gradually add the dashi stock and mirin. Whisk in the eggs and stir through the cabbage and spring onion.

Heat 1 teaspoon of the oil in a non-stick frying pan. Arrange one-quarter of the pork in the frying pan, forming a 12 cm (4½ in) circle. Cook for 1 minute, or until just starting to brown. Pour over one-quarter of the batter so that it just covers the pork. Cook on medium–high heat for 2 minutes, or until bubbles start to appear. Use a spatula to turn over. Brush with 1 tablespoon of the tonkatsu sauce, then continue to cook for a further 1–2 minutes, or until cooked through. Transfer to a plate and cover with foil to keep warm. Repeat this process with the remaining oil, pork, batter and tonkatsu sauce.

To serve, scatter the bonito flakes and nori over the okonomiyaki and drizzle with the mayonnaise.

Makes 4

chicken karaage

marinade
60 ml (2 fl oz/¼ cup) Japanese
   soy sauce
2 tablespoons mirin
1 tablespoon Japanese rice
   vinegar
2 teaspoons finely grated ginger

600 g (1 lb 5 oz) boneless,
   skinless chicken thigh
125 g (4½ oz/1 cup) potato
   flour
canola oil, for frying
1 tablespoon nori flakes
lemon wedges, to serve

To make the marinade, combine all the ingredients in a small bowl.

Cut the chicken into six 3–4 cm (1¼–1½ in) pieces and put in a large bowl. Add the marinade and toss to coat the chicken. Place in the fridge to marinate for 1 hour.

Remove the chicken from the marinade. Put the flour in a bowl. Toss several pieces of chicken in the flour to coat and transfer to a plate. Repeat with the remaining chicken.

Half fill a wok or deep frying pan with the oil and place over medium-high heat. When the surface of the oil is shimmering, add a piece of chicken. If the chicken sizzles on contact, the oil is ready. Add half of the chicken and fry for 4–5 minutes, or until golden. Remove with a slotted spoon and transfer to some paper towel to drain. Allow the oil to reheat, then fry the remaining chicken.

Scatter over the nori flakes and serve with the lemon wedges on the side.

Serves 4

onigiri with tuna and japanese tartare

japanese tartare
90 g (3¼ oz/⅓ cup) Japanese
    mayonnaise
2 cornichons (gherkins), finely chopped
1 spring onion (scallion), finely chopped

440 g (15½ oz/2 cups) Japanese
    short-grain rice
85 g (15 oz) tinned tuna, in brine
2 sheets nori
Japanese soy sauce, to serve

To make the tartare, combine all the ingredients in a small bowl.

Wash the rice in a sieve under cold running water. Put the rice and 685 ml (23½ fl oz/2¾ cups) cold water in a small, heavy-based saucepan and bring to the boil over high heat. Cover with a tight fitting lid, reduce the heat to low and cook for 15 minutes. Remove from the heat, fluff the rice with a spatula or large spoon and cover with a clean tea towel. Set aside for 15 minutes.

Put the tuna in a sieve over a bowl and press out as much water as possible. Transfer the tuna to a bowl and use a fork to finely flake. Stir through the tartare.

Line a teacup with plastic wrap, making sure it hangs over the side. Brush the plastic wrap with water. Gently press 1 loosely packed cup of rice into the teacup. Use a finger to make an indentation in the centre of the rice and put 1 teaspoon of the tuna mixture into the indentation. Draw the sides of the plastic wrap over the rice, remove from the teacup and firmly twist to enclose the rice. Keep twisting until the rice forms a ball. Repeat this process to make another five rice balls (avoid using any hardened rice on the base of the saucepan). Leave the rice wrapped in the plastic and set aside for 30 minutes.

Cut the sheets of nori into six 8 cm (3¼ in) squares.

Unwrap the rice balls and place each one on a square of nori. Serve with soy sauce.

Makes 6

slow-cooked pork belly

500 g (1 lb 2 oz) boneless pork
    belly, rind trimmed and cut
    into 4 cm (1½ in) pieces
2 teaspoons oil
1 small carrot, peeled and sliced
    into 2 cm (¾ in) thick rounds
150 g (5½ oz) daikon, cut into
    2 cm (¾ in) pieces
250 ml (9 fl oz/1 cup) dashi stock
60 ml (2 fl oz/¼ cup) sake

60 ml (2 fl oz/¼ cup) Japanese
    soy sauce
1½ tablespoons mirin
1½ tablespoons caster
    (superfine) sugar
1 tablespoon julienned ginger
3 tablespoons red miso
Japanese mustard, to serve
steamed rice, optional, to serve

Bring a large saucepan of water to a simmer. Place the pork belly
in a bamboo steamer and sit over the saucepan. Cover tightly and
steam for 1½ hours, or until the pork is nearly tender.

Heat the oil in a saucepan over medium–high heat. Add the pork
and cook for 3 minutes, or until golden. Add the carrot and daikon
and stir to coat. Add the dashi stock, sake, soy sauce, mirin,
sugar and ginger. Cook, uncovered, for 30 minutes, or until the
pork is tender.

Combine the miso with 1 tablespoon of water. Add to the pork and
stir to dissolve.

Serve with the Japanese mustard and bowls of rice, if desired.

Serves 4

fish steamed with miso and mirin

4 tablespoons white miso
80 ml (2½ fl oz/⅓ cup) mirin
2 teaspoons Japanese soy sauce
4 x 150 g (5½ oz) firm white
    fish fillets

1 spring onion (scallion), green
    part only, thinly sliced into
    lengths

Combine the miso, mirin and soy sauce in a small bowl.

Wash the fish fillets and pat dry. Put the fish in a flat ceramic dish and rub all over with the miso mixture. Place in the fridge to marinate for 3–6 hours.

Half fill a wok or large saucepan with water and bring to the boil. Line a bamboo steamer with baking paper and place the fish in the steamer, making sure the pieces do not touch.

Sit the steamer on the wok or saucepan, cover tightly and steam for 10 minutes, or until the fish flakes easily.

Sprinkle over the spring onion and serve.

Serves 4

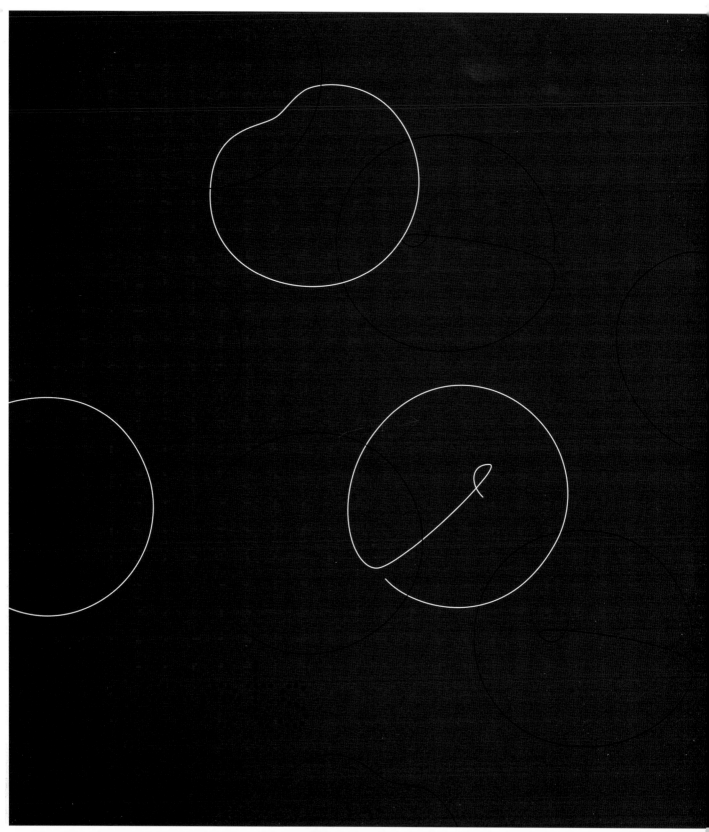

brown rice tea ice-cream

3 tablespoons brown rice tea
3 egg yolks
230 g (8 oz/1 cup) caster (superfine)
  sugar

500 ml (17 fl oz/2 cups) cream
cherries, optional, to serve

Put the brown rice tea in a heatproof bowl and pour over 250 ml (9 fl oz/1 cup) boiling water. Set aside for 10 minutes to allow the flavours to infuse. Strain the tea into a small bowl and discard the leaves.

Put the egg yolks in a heatproof bowl and whisk.

Put the sugar and half of the cream in a small saucepan and cook, stirring, over low heat for 5 minutes to dissolve the sugar.

Gradually pour the cream and sugar onto the egg yolks, whisking until well combined. Pour into a clean saucepan and cook over low heat for 8–10 minutes, stirring constantly, until the mixture coats the back of a wooden spoon. Do not allow the custard mixture to boil.

Pour the custard mixture into a bowl. Lay a piece of plastic wrap over the top to prevent a skin from forming. Allow to cool.

Add the tea and the remaining cream to the custard mixture, stirring well to combine. Pour the mixture into an ice-cream machine and churn until firm. Transfer to a small container, cover and freeze.

If you don't have an ice-cream machine, pour the mixture into a shallow tray, cover and freeze for 2 hours. Scrape the mixture into a bowl, beat with electric beaters until smooth. Return to the tray and freeze for another 2 hours. Repeat this process several more times until the ice-cream is very firm.

Serve with the cherries, if desired.

Serves 4

sesame mousse with red beans

130 g (4½ oz/¼ cup) tinned, sweet
    red beans
500 ml (17 fl oz/2 cups) cream
155 g (5½ oz/1 cup) toasted sesame
    seeds
1½ teaspoons powdered gelatine

220 g (7¾ oz/1 cup) sugar
3 eggs, separated
1 teaspoon vanilla extract
125 ml (4 fl oz/½ cup) cream, extra
1 teaspoon kinako (toasted sesame seed
    powder), optional

Spoon the red beans into six serving glasses and place in the fridge until needed.

Combine the cream and sesame seeds in a saucepan and place over medium heat. Just before the cream comes to a simmer, remove from the heat and set aside for 20 minutes. Strain the cream through a fine sieve, discarding the seeds.

Sprinkle the gelatine powder over 3 tablespoons of cold water while whisking with a fork. Set aside for 5 minutes, or until spongy. Stir the mixture through the warm cream mixture until smooth.

Beat the sugar, egg yolks and vanilla until the mixture is very thick. Pour 60 ml (2 fl oz/¼ cup) of the warm cream mixture into the egg mixture and beat to combine. Add the remaining cream mixture, beating well to combine.

Working quickly, beat the extra cream until firm. Beat the egg whites until they form firm peaks. Use a large metal spoon to fold the whipped cream into the cream mixture. Fold through the egg whites until the mixture is smooth.

Spoon the mousse over the chilled red beans and place in the fridge for 6 hours, or until set.

Serves 6

white peach strudel

4 large white peaches
1 teaspoon finely grated lemon zest
2 tablespoons lemon juice
1 tablespoon sake
55 g (2 oz/¼ cup) caster (superfine) sugar
30 g (1 oz/½ cup) panko (Japanese
    breadcrumbs)

2 teaspoons cornflour (cornstarch)
130 g (4½ oz/8 sheets) filo pastry
100 g (5½ oz) unsalted butter, melted
30 g (1 oz/¼ cup) icing (confectioners')
    sugar
3 tablespoons toasted sesame seeds
thick (double) cream, optional, to serve

Preheat the oven to 180°C (350°F/Gas 4). Line a baking tray with baking paper.

Cut the peaches in half and remove the stone. Finely slice the peaches and combine in a bowl with the lemon zest, lemon juice, sake, sugar, panko and cornflour. Set aside.

Working quickly to prevent the filo pastry from drying, lay a sheet of pastry on a clean work surface. Brush all over with about 1 tablespoon of the melted butter. Lay another sheet of filo on top and brush with another tablespoon of butter. Repeat this process until all the pastry has been used, brushing the final sheet of pastry with butter.

With one long end of the pastry closest to you, spoon the peach mixture parallel to the end closest to you in a neat and even log, leaving a 5 cm (2 in) space from the bottom and sides. Starting with the end nearest you, roll the pastry up and over the peaches to enclose. Tuck in the sides and continue rolling to form a large log.

Place the strudel on the prepared tray seam-side down and brush all over with the remaining butter. Sift the icing sugar on top and scatter over the sesame seeds. Bake for 45 minutes, or until the pastry is golden and the icing sugar has caramelised.

Allow to cool for a few minutes before slicing and serving with the cream, if desired.

Serves 4–6

nashi poached in plum wine

750 ml (26 fl oz/3 cups) umeshu
   (plum wine)
230 g (8 oz/1 cup) caster
   (superfine) sugar

1 vanilla bean
1 tablespoon lemon juice
4 nashi

Combine the umeshu and sugar in a saucepan. Rub the vanilla bean between the palms of your hands to soften. Use a small, sharp knife to cut the bean down the centre and scrape the vanilla seeds directly into the saucepan. Bring the mixture to the boil over medium–high heat, then reduce the heat and leave to simmer while you prepare the nashi.

Fill a bowl with cold water and add the lemon juice. Peel the nashi, slice in half and remove any seeds. Put the nashi in the lemon water as you go to prevent discolouring.

Drain the nashi and add to the poaching liquid. Simmer for about 15–20 minutes, or until the nashi are tender. Allow to cool a little in the poaching liquid before serving.

Serves 4

sake and melon granita

115 g (4 oz/½ cup) caster
(superfine) sugar
250 g (9 oz) honeydew melon,
finely chopped

250 ml (9 fl oz/1 cup) sake
250 ml (9 fl oz/1 cup) Midori
melon liqueur

Combine the sugar, melon and 500 ml (17 fl oz/2 cups) water in a saucepan. Bring to the boil over high heat, then reduce the heat to medium and cook for 10 minutes, stirring often, until the sugar is dissolved and the melon is starting to break up. Allow to cool, then strain through a fine sieve into a bowl. Stir through the sake and Midori, then pour into a 30 x 20 cm (12 x 8 in) tray and cover.

Put the tray in the freezer for 1½–2 hours, or until the mixture starts to freeze around the edge. Use a fork to stir the mixture, then return to the freezer for a further 30 minutes. Repeat this process every 30 minutes until the mixture is evenly icy and firm.

To serve, fluff the granita with a fork and spoon into glasses or small bowls.

Serves 4

green tea jelly

2 teaspoons matcha (green tea
   powder)
1 tablespoon gelatine powder
230 g (8 oz/1 cup) caster
   (superfine) sugar

blueberries, to serve
honeydew melon, to serve
cream, to serve

Put the matcha in a small bowl. Add 125 ml (4 fl oz/½ cup) boiling
water and stir until the matcha has dissolved. Set aside.

Sprinkle the gelatine powder over 3 tablespoons of cold water while
whisking with a fork. Set aside for 5 minutes, or until spongy.

Pour 475 ml (16½ fl oz) water into a saucepan. Add the matcha liquid
and sugar. Cook over low heat, stirring, for 3–5 minutes, or until the
sugar is dissolved and the syrup is warm.

Add the gelatine mixture to the saucepan and stir until dissolved.

Pour the mixture into six 100 ml (3½ fl oz) jelly (jello) moulds and place
in the fridge for 3–6 hours, or until set.

Serve with the blueberries, cubes of honeydew melon and cream.

Makes 6

chocolate truffles with soy bean powder

200 g (7 oz) dark chocolate,
    preferably Japanese, chopped
125 g (4½ oz) unsalted butter,
    chopped

1 tablespoon espresso coffee
100 ml (3½ fl oz) cream
2 tablespoons kinako
    (roasted soy bean flour)

Put the chocolate, butter, coffee and cream in a heatproof bowl.
Set the bowl over a saucepan of simmering water, making sure the
bottom of the bowl does not come into contact with the water. Heat
until the chocolate has softened, then stir until the mixture is smooth
and glossy. Remove from the heat and transfer to a bowl. Place in
the fridge for 3–6 hours, or until chilled and firm.

Dip a tablespoon into warm water. Use the warm spoon to scoop
out the chocolate mixture and transfer directly to a chilled serving
plate. Repeat this process to make eight truffles.

Sift the kinako over the truffles to serve.

Serves 6

green tea candied chestnuts

24 chestnuts
215 g (7¾ oz/1 cup) caster
    (superfine) sugar

1 tablespoon green tea leaves
vanilla ice-cream, optional,
    to serve

Preheat the oven to 220°C (425°F/Gas 7).

Use a small, sharp knife to cut a cross in the top of each chestnut. Put the chestnuts on a baking tray and bake for 20 minutes, or until they split open. Set aside until cool enough to handle, then peel.

Combine the chestnuts, sugar, tea leaves and 500 ml (17 fl oz/2 cups) water in a large saucepan over medium–high heat. Bring to the boil, stirring to dissolve the sugar. Reduce the heat to low–medium, then partially cover and simmer for 1 hour, or until slightly thickened.

Use tongs to transfer the chestnuts to a heatproof bowl. Strain over the sugar syrup, then set aside to cool slightly. Cover and place in the fridge for 2 hours to cool completely.

Serve the chestnuts with the ice-cream, if desired.

Serves 6

mochi

100 g (3½ oz/1 cup) glutinous
    rice flour
55 g (2 oz/¼ cup) caster
    (superfine) sugar
125 ml (4 fl oz/½ cup) milk

glutinous rice flour, extra,
    for dusting
90 g (3¼ oz/¼ cup) red bean
    paste

Combine the flour and sugar in a bowl. Make a well in the centre
and gradually add the milk, whisking with a fork, until a paste forms.
Pour onto a lightly greased plate.

Bring a large saucepan of water to a simmer. Place the plate in
a bamboo steamer and sit over the saucepan. Cover tightly and
steam for 20 minutes, or until the mixture is no longer sticky to
touch. Set aside for 5 minutes to cool slightly.

Lightly sprinkle your work surface with the extra rice flour. Divide the
mixture into four pieces and use a rolling pin to roll each one into a
10 cm (4 in) circle. Place 1 tablespoon of the red bean paste in the
centre of each circle and pull up the edge to enclose. Pinch to seal
and roll in the palms of your hands until smooth.

Dust the mochi with a little more rice flour to serve.

Makes 4

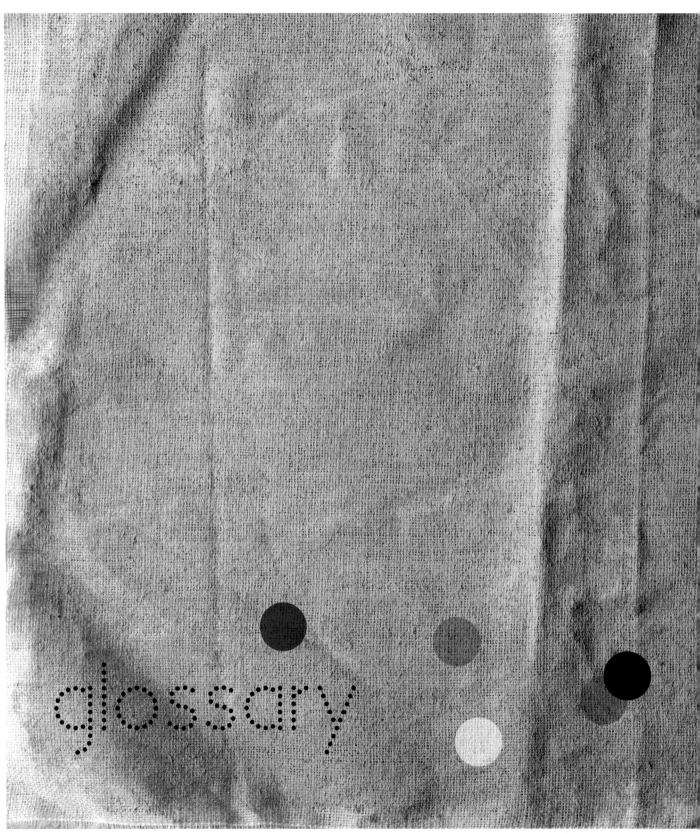

glossary

aonori flakes

Translating as 'blue/green seaweed', aonori comes from a different variety of seaweed to the nori used in sushi. The flakes are often found in shichimi spice mix and are also used as a seasoning on their own. Essential sprinkled on okonomiyaki.

bonito flakes

Salted and dried bonito fish adds depth and complexity in the form of dashi broth (where it is combined with dried kombu kelp) for many dressings, sauces and soups, including miso soup. Bonito can be purchased in whole dried fillets and shaved at home, or can be purchased already flaked. Fine flakes can be sprinkled directly onto food as a seasoning.

brown rice tea

Called genmaicha, this mixture of green tea leaves and roasted rice makes a mild, toasty, savoury brew. Some of the rice grains pop in the roasting process, so the tea looks like it contains small pieces of popcorn.

chilli oil

This modern addition to the Japanese pantry is served with Chinese-influenced dishes such as gyoza and ramen (noodle soups). At a basic level it is oil spiked with dried chilli flakes, but newer varieties include extra ingredients such as garlic, onion and sesame seeds.

daikon

This large, long white radish can be simmered like carrot until it reaches a mild, earthy sweetness, or can be cut finely and used crunchy and raw in salads or pickles.

dashi granules

Dashi broth is traditionally made with shavings of dried bonito fish and pieces of dried kombu kelp, but instant dashi granules are readily available in sachets or jars and just need to be mixed with water for a quick and flavoursome broth or base for sauces and dressings.

edamame beans

These fresh, young soybeans are served as a simple snack boiled in their pods with sea salt – you squeeze the nutty beans straight from the pods into your mouth. Podded beans can also be added to soups and salads. Whole and podded beans are sold frozen at Asian supermarkets.

gingko nuts

The nuts of gingko bilboa trees come inside a smooth cream shell not unlike a pistachio. Cracking them reveals a yellow nut with a papery brown skin, easily removed by blanching as you would an almond. However, gingko nuts can also be purchased already shelled, either vacuum-packed or frozen. They have a faint bittersweet flavour.

glutinous rice flour

The flour made from glutinous white rice lends a sticky, chewy consistency to many Asian sweets, including Japan's rice-flour cakes called mochi.

gow gee or gyoza wrappers

Packets of thin, round pastry skins called gow gee or gyoza wrappers can be found in the refrigerator section of Asian supermarkets. While the pastry can be made at home from flour and water, pre-made wrappers take away the labour of rolling.

green tea noodles

Green tea noodles – cha soba – are buckwheat noodles that have been flavoured and coloured with powdered green tea (matcha). Like regular soba noodles, they are sold in packets containing several straight, neat bundles that are each roughly an individual serve.

ichimi powder

Ichimi togarashi – literally 'one-flavour chilli' – is Japanese chilli powder, sold in small jars. It is related in name to shichimi togarashi – 'seven-flavour chilli' (see Shichimi Spice Mix).

Japanese mayonnaise

After production began in Japan in the early 20th century, mayonnaise has quickly grown in popularity to become a much-loved condiment. Their egg-rich version is made with oil such as soybean oil, and with rice or cider vinegar, and is sold in squeeze bottles.

Japanese mustard

Alongside the flavour of wasabi, it is easy to see how mustard – karashi – fits in with Japanese food. The Japanese style of mustard is relatively hot. It is generally sold in small tubes, but can also be purchased as a powder that is mixed with water.

Japanese rice vinegar

Rice vinegar from Japan is milder than Chinese varieties, which are in turn milder than most vinegars from the West. It adds essential sourness to sushi rice.

Japanese short-grain rice

The rice favoured across Japan is short-grain and has a sticky quality, making it easy to eat with chopsticks. It is available at most supermarkets.

Japanese soy sauce

Called shoyu, Japanese soy sauce is naturally fermented and aged. It is made from soybeans, wheat and salt. Tamari is another variety of soy sauce that is wheat-free.

kamaboko (fish cake)

This processed product is based on a paste of white fish, which is shaped into small loaves and steamed, and sold in plastic packages to be sliced at home. Kamaboko is popular in noodle soups and one-pot dishes.

kinako (roasted soy bean flour)

Whole soy beans are roasted and ground to give this flour a nutty flavour reminiscent of peanut butter. It can be used in baking and drinks, and can even be sprinkled directly onto food. In Japan it also turns up in Kit Kats.

lotus root

Fresh lotus roots can be found at Asian markets and are shaped like sweet potatoes, but are white. They are the rhizomes of a water lily, and slicing them into cross sections reveals a striking pattern of circular holes.

matcha (green tea powder)

This unique Japanese tea is made by grinding high-quality tea leaves to a powder. It is mixed with water in individual cups to produce a vibrant spinach-coloured brew and is served at traditional tea ceremonies. It can also be used to make delicious sweets and ice-cream.

mirin

This sweet rice wine has a reduced alcohol content compared to sake and is used in cooking, such as in marinades. The label on the bottle often describes it as 'sake for cooking'. It is available from most supermarkets.

miso

This classic Japanese ingredient is made from soy beans, salt, and rice or barley. It is fermented and ground to a strong savoury paste. There are several varieties such as white miso, which is sweet, and red miso, which is full-flavoured. They all add unique body and flavour to Japanese soups, marinades and dressings.

mizuna

This salad green with feathered leaves (similar to rocket) has a mildly spicy mustard flavour. It is used in salads and soups.

nori

Fresh algae from the sea is cut finely and mixed to a paste, then spread into paper-thin sheets to dry. The sheets are cut into squares the right size for wrapping sushi rolls, but can also be cut into fine shreds and used as a delicate garnish.

panko (Japanese breadcrumbs)

Japanese breadcrumbs are making inroads into non-Asian cooking because of their light and flaky texture that becomes crisp but not overloaded with oil when fried. They can be found at most supermarkets.

pickled ginger

With its sweet, hot, cleansing flavour, pickled ginger is a regular accompaniment to sushi. It is made with rice vinegar, sugar, salt and young ginger, which naturally blushes light pink as it pickles – although commercial varieties often contain colouring.

ponzu sauce

This is a mixture of citrus juice (such as from the Japanese fruit yuzu), rice vinegar and mirin, flavoured with kombu kelp and bonito – and often with soy sauce added too. Ponzu sauce can be made at home (see page 66) or purchased in bottles.

potato flour

This flour is used to thicken soups and sauces, and to dust onto ingredients before deep-frying for a crisp coating.

red bean paste

This sweet paste made from adzuki beans is one of the star ingredients of Japanese desserts, which often blur the Western division between sweet and savoury. It is found in tins, but can also be made at home.

sake

The traditional alcoholic drink of Japan is a clear liquid brewed from rice. With a relatively high alcohol content of around 20 per cent, it is drunk from small cups, and is sometimes served warm. In cooking it is often used in marinades such as teriyaki.

sesame oil

Toasted sesame oil may be known as a Chinese ingredient, but it is also much used in Japan. It has a fragrant, nutty flavour that livens up salad dressings and marinades even when only added in small quantities.

sesame seeds

Toasted sesame seeds ground in a suribachi (mortar and pestle) form the base of many Japanese sauces and dressings. White sesame seeds are the most common, while the more unusual black seeds have a stronger flavour and are often used as a garnish.

shichimi spice mix

This 'seven-flavour' mixture is an interesting blend of ingredients (not necessarily seven) including chilli, citrus peel, sansho peppercorns (Japan's species of sichuan pepper), black and/or white sesame seeds, aonori flakes, hemp seeds, white poppy seeds and ginger, and sometimes also including shiso and mustard seeds. It is sprinkled on top of soups and noodles and can be purchased in small jars.

shiitake mushrooms

The meaty, flavoursome character of shiitake mushrooms is adored in Japan, and used in countless dishes. If fresh is unavailable, dried shiitake can be rehydrated in water – and the water leftover can be used as a lightly flavoured stock.

shiso leaves

Known as perilla in English, this herb has serrated leaves like large nettles and comes in either green or purple. Its distinctively musty fragrance and taste has notes of mint and cumin, and it is used in pickles and tempura and mixed with rice.

silken tofu

This soft, undrained tofu (made from soy bean milk and a coagulant) needs to be treated with care so it doesn't fall apart, but is loved for its luscious velvety texture.

soba (buckwheat) noodles

These brownish-grey noodles can be made with 100 per cent buckwheat flour, but often contain a little wheat flour as well. They are delicious in soups and cold salads with flavoursome dressings or dipping sauces.

suribachi

Japan's version of the mortar and pestle is wider and shallower compared to other mortars, and has a wooden pestle. The bowl is glazed ceramic on the outside and unglazed on the inside with tiny grooves to assist grinding.

sweet red beans

While commonly blended to a paste, cooked red (adzuki) beans sweetened with sugar are also sold whole in tins, ready to be made into desserts such as the soup called oshiruko. If tinned is unavailable, you can cook sweet red beans at home.

tonkatsu sauce

'Tonkatsu' translates to 'pork cutlet', as this sauce is famously served with crumbed, deep-fried pork. The sauce is described as Japanese worcestershire – but it is thicker, has no anchovies, and is fruitier with ingredients such as apples, tomatoes and prunes.

umeboshi (pickled plum) paste

Ume plums (more closely related to apricots) are picked under-ripe and are salted in barrels, with purple shiso often added to colour them red. After several months they are set to dry, creating shrivelled, puckered plums that are popular with rice for breakfast. The paste made from their flesh is used for sauces and dressings.

umeshu (plum wine)

Under-ripe ume plums are steeped in alcohol and sugar to make a drink with a refreshing light sour note. It is served over ice in summer.

wakame

This seaweed is used in soups such as miso soup, and in salads. It is sold dried in whole pieces or shredded, and quickly softens in cold water.

wasabi

'Japanese horseradish' is a gnarled green root with a powerful hot flavour, grated as a condiment for sushi. Outside Japan, it is mostly found as a ready-made paste in small tubes.

won ton wrappers

Won ton wrappers are square yellow pastry skins made of flour and eggs. They are found in packets in the refrigerator section of Asian supermarkets.

index

A

agedashi tofu 119
asparagus
    crumbed asparagus 26
    grilled beef stuffed with asparagus 37
    prosciutto and asparagus skewers 89

B

beans
    green beans with black sesame dressing 61
    green beans with miso 21
beef
    beef and spring onion skewers 90
    beef teriyaki 101
    grilled beef stuffed with asparagus 37
brown rice tea ice-cream 150

C

cabbage
    cabbage salad with sesame dressing 65
    pork and cabbage gyoza 112
    spring onion and cabbage okonomiyaki 46
camembert tempura 41
cheese
    camembert tempura 41
    fried pork stuffed with cheese 22
    tempura cheese-stuffed chillies 30
chicken
    chicken balls 105
    chicken karaage 140
    chicken nanban 42
    chicken and shiitake skewers 78
    chicken skewers with sake and soy 93
    tatsuya fried chicken 132
chilli
    chilli prawns 82
    tempura cheese-stuffed chillies 30
chocolate truffles with soy bean powder 162
clams, sake-steamed, with soy butter 131
crab
    crab croquettes 136
    crab and wakame salad 57
    soft-shell crab salad with ponzu 66
crisp pork belly skewers 106
croquettes
    crab 136
    potato 120

crumbed asparagus 26
crumbed prawns 18
custards, steamed savoury 123

D

daikon and wakame salad 54
deep-fried eggplant sandwiches 33
deep-fried oysters with tonkatsu 38
duck with umeboshi 98

E

edamame salad with miso dressing 70
eggplant
    deep-fried eggplant sandwiches 33
    eggplant with miso 116
    grilled eggplant with soy and ginger 135
eggs
    pork okonomiyaki 139
    spring onion and cabbage okonomiyaki 46
    sweet egg omelette 34

F

fish cake skewers 102
fish steamed with miso and mirin 147
fritters, vegetable and prawn 29

G

green beans with black sesame dressing 61
green beans with miso 21
green salad with creamy dressing 53
green tea candied chestnuts 165
green tea jelly 161
green tea noodle salad 69
gyoza
    pork and cabbage 112
    vegetable 128

I

ice-cream, brown rice tea 150

J

Japanese pickles 13
Japanese-style potato salad 50

L

lotus chips 10
lotus root salad 62

M

miso
edamame salad with miso dressing 70
eggplant with miso 116
fish steamed with miso and mirin 147
green beans with miso 21
miso-glazed salmon skewers 109
mochi 166
mushrooms
chicken and shiitake skewers 78
shiitake and sesame skewers 94

N

nashi poached in plum wine 157
noodles
green tea noodle salad 69
soba noodle salad 58

O

okonomiyaki
pork 139
spring onion and cabbage 46
omelette, sweet egg 34
onigiri with salmon and bonito 124
onigiri with tuna and Japanese tartare 143
onigiri with umeboshi and tofu 115
oysters
deep-fried oysters with tonkatsu 38
oysters with Japanese dressing 14

P

pickles, Japanese 13
ponzu sauce 66
pork
crisp pork belly skewers 106
fried pork stuffed with cheese 22
pork and cabbage gyoza 112
pork okonomiyaki 139
pork skewers with umeboshi 97
slow-cooked pork belly 144
potatoes
Japanese-style potato salad 50
potato croquettes 120
prawns
chilli prawns 82
crumbed prawns 18
steamed savoury custards 123

vegetable and prawn fritters 29
prosciutto and asparagus skewers 89

R

rice
onigiri with salmon and bonito 124
onigiri with tuna and Japanese tartare 143
onigiri with umeboshi and tofu 115

S

sake and melon granita 158
sake-steamed clams with soy butter 131
salads
cabbage salad with sesame dressing 65
crab and wakame salad 57
daikon and wakame salad 54
edamame salad with miso dressing 70
green beans with black sesame dressing 61
green salad with creamy dressing 53
green tea noodle salad 69
Japanese-style potato salad 50
lotus root salad 62
soba noodle salad 58
soft-shell crab salad with ponzu 66
salmon
miso-glazed salmon skewers 109
onigiri with salmon and bonito 124
savoury custards, steamed 123
scallops
grilled scallops with nori 86
scallops with ginger and mirin 127
seafood
chilli prawns 82
crab croquettes 136
crab and wakame salad 57
crumbed prawns 18
deep-fried oysters with tonkatsu 38
fish cake skewers 102
fish steamed with miso and mirin 147
fried squid with lemon and salt 25
grilled scallops with nori 86
grilled squid with soy and mirin 77
miso-glazed salmon skewers 109
onigiri with salmon and bonito 124
onigiri with tuna and Japanese tartare 143
oysters with Japanese dressing 14
sake-steamed clams with soy butter 131

scallops with ginger and mirin 127
soft-shell crab salad with ponzu 66
steamed savoury custards 123
takoyaki 45
vegetable and prawn fritters 29

sesame
cabbage salad with sesame dressing 65
green beans with black sesame dressing 61
sesame mousse with red beans 153
shiitake and sesame skewers 94
spinach with sesame 17
shiitake and sesame skewers 94

skewers
beef and spring onion skewers 90
beef teriyaki 101
chicken balls 105
chicken and shiitake skewers 78
chicken skewers with sake and soy 93
chilli prawns 82
crisp pork belly skewers 106
duck with umeboshi 98
fish cake skewers 102
grilled scallops with nori 86
grilled squid with soy and mirin 77
marinated tofu skewers 81
miso-glazed salmon skewers 109
pork skewers with umeboshi 97
prosciutto and asparagus skewers 89
shiitake and sesame skewers 94
spring onion skewers 85
tofu and vegetable skewers 74

slow-cooked pork belly 144
soba noodle salad 58
soft-shell crab salad with ponzu 66

soy
chicken nanban 42
chicken skewers with sake and soy 93
grilled eggplant with soy and ginger 135
sake-steamed clams with soy butter 131

spinach with sesame 17

spring onions
beef and spring onion skewers 90
spring onion and cabbage okonomiyaki 46
spring onion skewers 85

squid
fried squid with lemon and salt 25
grilled squid with soy and mirin 77

sweet egg omelette 34

sweets
brown rice tea ice-cream 150
chocolate truffles with soy bean powder 162
green tea candied chestnuts 165
green tea jelly 161
mochi 166
nashi poached in plum wine 157
sake and melon granita 158
sesame mousse with red beans 153
white peach strudel 154

T
takoyaki 45
tatsuya fried chicken 132

tempura
camembert tempura 41
tempura cheese-stuffed chillies 30

teriyaki beef 101

tofu
agedashi tofu 119
marinated tofu skewers 81
onigiri with umeboshi and tofu 115
tofu and vegetable skewers 74

U
umeboshi
duck with umeboshi 98
onigiri with umeboshi and tofu 115
pork skewers with umeboshi 97

V
vegetable gyoza 128
vegetable and prawn fritters 29

W
wakame
crab and wakame salad 57
daikon and wakame salad 54

white peach strudel 154

Published in 2011 by Hardie Grant Books

Hardie Grant Books (Australia)
85 High Street
Prahran, Victoria 3181
www.hardiegrant.com.au

Hardie Grant Books (UK)
Second Floor, North Suite
Dudley House
Southampton Street
London WC2E 7HF
www.hardiegrant.co.uk

National Library of Australia Cataloguing-in-Publication Data:
Title: Izakaya : Japanese bar food.
ISBN: 9781742700427 (pbk.)
Subjects: Cooking, Japanese.
Snack foods--Japan.
Dewey Number: 641.5952

Publisher: Paul McNally
Editor: Jane Winning
Design, illustrations and layout: Michelle Mackintosh
Photographer: Chris Chen
Stylist: Vanessa Austin
Recipes: Ross Dobson and Alison Adams
Additional text: Rachel Pitts
Colour reproduction by Splitting Image Colour Studio
Printed in China by 1010 Printing International Limited

The publisher would like to thank the following for their generosity
in supplying props for the book: Japan City (Bondi Junction),
Porters Paints, Dulux, Jstyle and Mud Australia.